THE QUOTABLE TYCOON

THE QUOTABLE TYCOON

AN IRREVERENT COLLECTION OF
Brutally Honest
and **Inspirational**
BUSINESS WISDOM

DAVID OLIVE

SOURCEBOOKS, INC.®
NAPERVILLE, ILLINOIS

Published by Sourcebooks, Inc.
P.O. Box 4410, Naperville, Illinois 60567-4410
(630) 961-3900
FAX: (630) 961-2168
www.sourcebooks.com

 Originally published in 2002.

Library of Congress Cataloging-in-Publication Data

Olive, David.
  The quotable tycoon : an irreverent collection of brutally honest and inspirational business wisdom / David Olive.
      p. cm.
 1. Business--Quotations, maxims, etc. I. Title.
PN6084.B87O44 2004
650--dc22

                                        2004013839

Printed and bound in the United States of America
BG 10 9 8 7 6 5 4 3 2

For Findlay Bergstra

He had flown up very high to see, on strong wings, when he was young. And while he was up there he had looked on all the kingdoms, with the kind of eyes that can stare straight into the sun.

F. Scott Fitzgerald, *The Last Tycoon*

You get up on your little 21-inch screen and howl about America and democracy. There is no America. There is no democracy. There is only IBM and AT&T and DuPont, Dow and Union Carbide, Exxon. Those are the nations of the world today…We no longer live in a world of nations and ideologies, Mr. Beale. The world is a college of corporations, inexorably determined by the immutable by-laws of business. The world *is* a business, Mr. Beale. It has been since man crawled out of the slime.

Paddy Chayevsky, *Network*

Acknowledgments

I wish to thank the staff of Pearson Canada for their assistance with this book. In particular, I wish to acknowledge the helpful counsel of editors Susan Folkins, Andrea Crozier and Marcia Miron, and the generosity of Kenneth Kidd and the *Toronto Star* for their support during the completion of the work.

Preface

"I'll go to jail rather than discuss my personal affairs," J. P. Morgan vowed some ninety years ago. Today the public and private lives of business tycoons are on open display. The unseen wizardry of J. P. Morgan, who quietly rescued the United States from more than one financial "panic," has long since given way to the highly publicized managerial sermons of Jack Welch, the cautionary investment tales of Warren Buffett, and the promotional antics of Donald Trump and Sir Richard Branson.

What gave rise to this cult of the celebrity CEO? The triumph of free-market forces over communism has pushed political heroes and villains to the sidelines, and we now look increasingly to private-sector leaders as the chief actors in our social drama. With the current unprecedented reliance of Main Street investors on a volatile stock market, the tycoons who create and destroy billions of dollars worth of retirement savings are scrutinized as never before.

Ballplayers and prime ministers can only envy the staying power of the most successful tycoons, whose unchallenged tenure gives them unrivaled influence over whole generations of would-be emulators. Welch's reign at General Electric, which spanned the terms of three U.S. presidents, saw the term "Neutron Jack" applied to any CEO who, like him, started out by drastically shrinking the payroll while leaving the company standing. Later, Welch's "rank and yank" practice of continually culling deadwood similarly entered the language and would become widely copied.

New expressions are also continually coined to describe spectacular flameouts, as demonstrated by the ouster of Kenneth Lay as CEO of Enron, the Houston-based energy-trading firm that became the biggest bankruptcy in U.S. history in 2001 amid charges of accounting flim-flammery. Only a year earlier, Lay had exhorted Enron employees to adhere to the most exacting standards of ethical behavior: "Enron's reputation finally depends on its people, on you and me—let's keep that reputation high," Lay wrote in the company's sixty-four-page code of conduct, which was later offered for sale as a collector's item on eBay (asking price: $160). Lay, too, became a universal symbol, in this case for companies where cooking the books and deceiving employees, shareholders, and regulators are everyday tools of the managerial trade. "Enronitis," for accounting shenanigans, and "Lay'd off," for foot soldiers made to pay the price for chi-

Goizueta, Enrico's longtime counterpart at Coca-Cola, tried to be sanguine about the potential for disaster in a corporate ethos that puts such a high premium on decisiveness. Goizueta, author of the epic "New Coke" flop in the mid-1980s, said, "Once you've made the philosophical decision not to commit suicide, you're committed to being an optimist." (Goizueta died of natural causes.)

Even the optimists watch their backs. Taking stock of his career as a monopolist who was demonized for his unrivaled power over an industry, John D. Rockefeller Sr. confessed in his memoir that each night when his head hit the pillow he said softly to himself, "Now a little success, soon you will fall down, soon you will be overthrown." This from a tycoon who never suffered a debilitating setback in a career that lasted half a century.

The fear level runs still higher among the not so fortunate. "We need to be paranoid optimists," said Robert Eaton, CEO of Chrysler, which more than once looked into the abyss. In the frenetic tech arena, where products have a shelf life of mere months before they are rendered obsolete by a surprise new offering from a previously unknown adversary, it's understandable that Candace Carpenter, founder of the Internet firm iVillage, would "go to sleep worrying someone's going to leave cleat marks on my face before I wake up." Andy Grove, one of the most accomplished tycoons of the 20th century, should be a contented man after leading Intel to world leadership in semiconductors. His memoir instead describes his constant anticipation of crisis, of the likelihood of being overtaken by events and upstart competitors. His title for the memoir, _Only the Paranoid Survive_, was immediately adopted as the motto for all Silicon Valley entrepreneurs.

The only thing more common than business leaders professing in Chamber of Commerce conclaves their ardent love of free markets is their less public voicing of their near universal anxiety over genuine competition. "It's like trying to screw an elephant," Henry Ford said in frustration as the Chevrolet division of General Motors overtook his once dominant firm. "This is rat eat rat, dog eat dog, I'll kill 'em and I'm going to kill 'em before they kill me," vowed McDonald's founder Ray Kroc, who also had this advice for his franchisees: "What do you do when your competitor's drowning? Get a live hose and stick it in his mouth."

There is a certain fraternalism among rival lawyers and basketball stars away from the courts; not so for rivals in business. "I don't like our competitors," said Hugh McColl, forsaking his expected role as an industry statesman after transforming the Bank of America into the industry's biggest player in the 1990s. "I don't eat with them, don't do anything with them except try to waste them." Is the lingerie market, of all things, a take-no-prisoners battleground? Why yes, says Leslie Wexner, founder of The Limited, the owner of innergarments marketer Victoria's Secret. "It is a war, and in wars

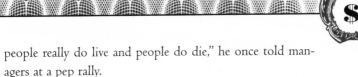

people really do live and people do die," he once told managers at a pep rally.

To be sure, kinder, gentler views have begun to intrude on the tycoon mentality in recent years. In the 1990s, Lew Platt, CEO of Hewlett-Packard, campaigned for a worker-friendly culture. Before giving way to successor Carly Fiorina at the behest of a board that thought he'd grown too soft, Platt complained that "one of our senior managers had a meeting with his staff to discuss work-life balance. The meeting started at five PM and ended at nine—and the manager didn't see the irony." It takes a certain resolve to overturn the feudal ways of conventional big business. A defiant Sir Marcus Sieff, CEO of British retailer Marks & Spencer, has noted, "There's a saying in the company that a senior executive is treated almost as well as a shop assistant or warehouseman. And anybody who says you can't do it in a company of this size is talking bullshit." But Eric Schmidt, for one, is uncomfortable with touchy-feely values. "I would be unhappy if people weren't whining," said the CEO of U.S. software leader Novell. "I want them to want more. The kind of mild dissatisfaction with what you have is a key prerequisite for success in business." How about the vaunted efforts to seamlessly integrate the cultures of merged enterprises? Charles Wang will have none of that. "I'm not blending cultures, I'm acquiring you," the CEO of U.S. software maker CA Associates tells employees of his newly purchased companies. "Look at your paycheck next month. I bet it says CA at the top left-hand corner."

The able tycoon is unsentimental about cutting his losses. "If you can't fix it, sell it," said Allen Born, CEO of U.S. mineral producer Amax, on how to deal with a badly performing division. "If you can't sell it, shoot it." At times one must have the gumption to shed all of one's problems in one go. CEO of AT&T, Charles Brown, had this explanation for recording a massive one-time write-off of billions of dollars worth of assets: "It is generally considered more comfortable to take a dog's tail off all at once rather than an inch at a time," he said.

Tycoons act with similar alacrity in dispensing with superfluous personnel. Granted, there is the question of how this drag on the bottom line came about in the first place. "Why did you get into a position that you had to lay off a bunch of people?" asks Livio DeSimone, CEO of 3M (formally known as Minnesota Mining & Manufacturing), a firm with an unwritten no-layoff policy. "How come you're so smart now that you've laid off a bunch of people?" But the more commonly accepted wisdom, championed by Welch, is that continual payroll pruning is essential to any firm hoping to achieve a global competitive advantage. "A company that bets its future on its people must remove that lower 10 percent," Welch says, "and keep removing it every year—always raising the bar of performance and increasing the quality of its leadership." Such workforce minimalism can go to extremes, as with Jeffrey Skilling, briefly CEO of the ill-fated Enron, whose Holy Grail was the "employee-light" operation.

"Depopulate," he said. "Get rid of people. They gum up the works."

What draws tycoons into their quest? For Bill Gates, it was nothing less, he has said, than a chance to revolutionize the world and to take his place alongside Robert Fulton, Karl Benz, and Alexander Graham Bell. For Steve Case, founder of America Online, it was the opportunity "to build a global medium as central to people's lives as the telephone or television—and even more valuable." Louis Renault, a protégé of Henry Ford, aimed to "construct the best cars at the lowest prices, so that one day every family in France can have its own little car."

With his sights set only a little lower, Samuel Curtis Johnson, of U.S. consumer products maker S. C. Johnson, takes pride in his sense of mission. "We are polishing the floors and furniture, cleaning the rug, killing the bugs, sweetening the air, and waxing the old man's car. And whenever you get bit by a mosquito, remember I'm smiling." William Wrigley acknowledged that his firm's noble purpose was to supply the world with a product that was essentially an "adult pacifier." Sizing up the market for multi-tasking goods, Martha Stewart has been almost apologetic about the ambit of her ambitions. "I don't mean to sound egomaniacal, but Perry Como used to own Christmas on TV," she said. "By 'own,' I mean monopolize and influence."

This is not a book for aspiring tycoons who don't especially like to be held up to the mirror. The caustic musings and durable aphorisms of these leaders yield insights of use for people in all walks of life. "Luck may help a man over a ditch—if he jumps well," is food-processing pioneer H. J. Heinz's handy reminder to be prepared. Makeup entrepreneur Estée Lauder warns that "when you're angry, never put it in writing. It's like carving your anger in stone. That makes implacable enemies." Boston land developer and media tycoon Mortimer Zuckerman cautions that "before you build a better mousetrap, it helps to know if there are any mice out there," a truism that eluded hundreds of failed dot-com adventurers. Get to know your lieutenants over drinks at after-hours clubs, offers Jurgen Schrempp, CEO of DaimlerChrysler and a notorious pub crawler, because "you never really hear the truth from your subordinates until after ten in the evening." Beware of management fads. "If you empower dummies," says Rick Teerlink, CEO of Harley-Davidson, "you get bad decisions faster." Thinking of bringing your brother-in-law into the business? Jack Warner took visitor Albert Einstein aside during a tour of the Warner Bros. studio. "I have a theory of relatives too," he told the scientist. "Don't hire 'em."

Does the tycoon lifestyle tempt you? Very well. But brace for the mighty influence you will have. Assessing his own impact on television, Ted Turner allows that "a full moon blanks out all the stars around it." Who knows, you might become a counselor to kings, a perennial cover-story profilee

in *Fortune* and owner of a yacht that can barely squeeze through the Panama Canal, all the while yoking the fate of countless wage slaves to your mercurial mind. But some things won't change. Says Warren Buffett, "If you were a jerk before, you'll be a bigger jerk with a billion dollars."

Absurdities

Nuclear war would really set back cable TV.
> TED TURNER, *U.S. media mogul, in the 1980s.*

It is now possible for a flight attendant to get a pilot pregnant.
> RICHARD J. FERRIS, *CEO of United Airlines, in the 1980s, when United became one of the world's first major carriers to recruit male flight attendants and female pilots.*

If people would only behave themselves, the price of tires would go down.
> ROBERT MERCER, *CEO of Goodyear Tire & Rubber, in 1988, on how the AIDS epidemic was increasing demand for rubber condoms and gloves, thus raising raw material costs for Goodyear.*

He wanted me to be Joseph Stalin. I told him I resented that. I wanted to be Winston Churchill, but he didn't want me to be that.
> JAMES BARKSDALE, *CEO of Netscape Communications, pioneer of the Navigator Web browser, in the mid-1990s, recalling a conversation with Steve Case, CEO of America Online, who styled himself and Barksdale as "the Allies" pitted against Microsoft's Explorer web browser.*

The nadir of this activity occurred at the end of last year's Hollinger International annual meeting, when a representative of a large New York house po-facedly asked me if we would lend him stock so he could short our stock further. Robust capitalist that I am, I found this reckless neanderthalism avarice distasteful.

CONRAD BLACK, *later Lord Black of Crossharbour, Anglo-Canadian press baron, recalling Hollinger's 1999 annual meeting.*

I have lived for 613,000 hours, 201,000 of them were in childhood, youth, and [a] thoroughly sort of inadequate education. That leaves 412,000. You take a third of that for sleep and rest. So I'm down to 275,000 hours. I take out a month for holidays, at least half a weekend, family time, evenings, etc., and you're down to, at the very maximum, a couple hundred thousand hours I've been at work. And then I go, What have I done? How much time have I wasted in endless meetings with no decisions? Industry conferences? Studying overlong reports? Yeah, I guess I've wasted at least half my life, so that gets me down to perhaps 100,000 useful hours. Pretty bad figures. So if I'm pretty healthy and have a normal life expectancy—I'm a bit of an optimist—I've got about another 175,000 hours to go, of which maybe I can spend 75,000 productively at work. All right? Or 70,000, say. So I've just got to see that each one of those hours is well spent.

RUPERT MURDOCH, *Australian American media baron, in a 2001 conference in New York.*

Accounting Practices

Be sure that you are not deceiving yourself at any time about actual conditions. Study the books and face the truth. We knew how much we made and where we gained or lost. At least, we tried not to deceive ourselves.

> JOHN D. ROCKEFELLER SR., *founder of U.S. oil giant Standard Oil, in the late 19th century.*

I know of no more deplorable mistake in business organizations, great or small, than that the men in charge should fool themselves as to the truth of their operations.

> SIR JOSEPH WESLEY FLAVELLE, *founder of Toronto-based food processor Canada Packers, in the early 20th century, on deceptive accounting practices at debt-burdened Canadian National Railways.*

The easiest way to do a snow job on investors (or on yourself) is to change one factor in the accounting each month. Then you can say, "It's not comparable with last month or last year. And we can't really draw any conclusions from the figures."

> ROBERT TOWNSEND, *CEO of Avis Rent-A-Car, in his 1970 book* Up the Organization.

When you find the source of the problem, you insist that management must manage to solve that problem. You don't

want them to manage by the numbers—pushing sales or receivables from one quarter to another. That is like treating the thermometer instead of the patient.

> **HAROLD GENEEN**, *longtime CEO of U.S. conglomerate ITT, in his 1984 memoir,* Managing.

There are North American accounting principles, European accounting principles, German accounting principles and Volkswagen accounting principles.

> **CARL HAHN**, *CEO of German automaker Volkswagen, in* Forbes *in 1990, acknowledging criticism from U.S. investors that his company's numbers were convoluted.*

REALITY CHECK

Two and two is four and five'll get you ten—if you know how to work it.

> **MAE WEST**

The financial consequences of [mistakes] are regularly dumped into massive restructuring charges or write-offs that are casually waved off as "nonrecurring." Managements just love these. Indeed, in recent years it has seemed that no earnings statement is complete without them. The origins of these charges, though, are never explored. When it comes to corporate blunders, CEOs invoke the concept of the Virgin Birth.

WARREN BUFFETT, *CEO of U.S. investment firm Berkshire Hathaway, in his 2001 letter to shareholders.*

Advancement

Anyone who advertises for a promotion is slitting his throat. The job has to seek the man. You don't get ahead by confrontation, but by demonstrating that someone misjudged you.

IRVING SHAPIRO, *CEO of DuPont, in the 1970s.*

I think the most important thing is to take a chance on people. Somebody took a hell of a chance on me.

WALTER WRISTON, *former CEO of Citicorp, in 1984.*

You have to be willing to challenge people and always advance them a little bit sooner than you think you should. We drill dry holes with people just like we drill dry holes looking for oil and gas.

JOHN BOOKOUT, *CEO of Anglo-Dutch oil producer Shell, in* Fortune *in 1987.*

Most CEOs got their jobs because their predecessors and the directors liked them. They slapped the right backs and laughed at the right jokes. It's reverse Darwinism: Once a backslapper gets the top job, he sure as hell isn't going to have somebody better than him as his heir apparent. So management gets worse and worse.

CARL C. ICAHN, *U.S. corporate raider, in* Fortune *in 1988.*

Women's networks do women zero good professionally. My advice is find a niche and then become the best there is in that field.

DARLA MOORE, *CEO of Texas investment firm Rainwater, in* Fortune *in 1996.*

My advice is to focus 100 percent on doing your job better than anybody else. I've seen a lot of highflying people fall flat because they were so focused on the next job, they didn't get the current job done.

CARLETON S. (CARLY) FIORINA, *CEO of Hewlett-Packard, in 2001.*

I always went into an area that was in last place, with a philosophy, "You can't fall off the floor."

MICHAEL D. EISNER, *CEO of Walt Disney Co., in the late 1990s, on picking tough assignments early in his career.*

Adversaries

I avoid bad luck by being patient. Whenever I am obliged to get into a fight, I always wait and let the other fellow get tired first.

> JAY GOULD, *19th-century U.S. railroad speculator.*

The only dirty trick I ever played on André Citroën was to show him my new factory on the Île de Seguin. After that he ruined himself trying to do in three months what had taken me thirty years to accomplish.

> LOUIS RENAULT, *French automaker, on his only major French rival. Citroën's effort to replicate Renault's modern factory with his own costly project at the Quai de Javel ruined the company in the 1940s.*

This is rat eat rat, dog eat dog, I'll kill 'em and I'm going to kill 'em before they kill me.

> RAY KROC, *founder of McDonald's, in the 1960s.*

To be successful in business you need friends. To be very successful, you need enemies.

> CHRISTOPHER ONDAATJE, *Ceylon-born Canadian financier and philanthropist, in the 1980s.*

Knowing yourself and your enemies is the first prerequisite to becoming a warrior.

> KEE KUN-HEE, *chairman of South Korean conglomerate Samsung, in* Business Week *in 1994.*

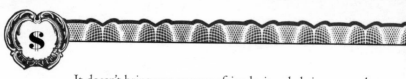

It doesn't bring you any new friends, it only brings you a better class of enemies.

> **ISRAEL HAROLD (IZZY) ASPER**, *Canadian broadcasting and newspaper magnate, in a 2002 television interview, on how he regards his life as a media baron.*

This has been my most successful year ever, and all those who've let me down have been calling and even going through intermediaries in order to have breakfast, lunch, dinner or "anything" with me. They are miraculously turning up on my doorstep seeking a second chance. I will leave them out in the rain; there can be no second chance for people who are disloyal, because they will only come back to bite you again. Their calls will go unanswered.

> **DONALD TRUMP**, *New York developer, in his essay "I'm Back" in the* New York Times Magazine *in 1995, a few years after he recovered from a reversal of fortune.*

Sometimes, people underestimate me…. That happened in my war with LVMH. Bernard Arnault, the chairman, thought he could walk all over me. But we never quit. People from Calabria eat nails for breakfast.

> **DOMENICO DE SOLE**, *CEO of Florence-based fashion marketer Gucci Group, in the* New York Times *in 2002, on his success in fending off a hostile takeover of Gucci by LVMH Moët Hennessey Louis Vuitton.*

Adversity

The Great Depression of the '30s tossed my own life's work from a tidy little mound of success into a bottomless pit of debts, humiliations, and mortgages. Men were jumping from hotel windows, *my* hotel windows, but Mother was perfectly calm. "Some men jump out of windows," she said. "Some go to church. Pray, Connie. It's the best investment you'll ever make."

> CONRAD HILTON, *in his 1957 memoir,* Be My Guest, *on the loss of a modest chain of hotels he assembled in the 1920s.*

When asked about publishing I describe the scene when you're walking in the moonlight in a beautiful garden, there's the scent of flowers, and everything's lovely. But in the dark, you step on the head of a rake and the handle comes up and hits you on the head. That's publishing.

> JACK MCCLELLAND, *CEO of Canadian book publisher McClelland & Stewart, in the 1970s.*

I used to own forty thousand turkeys. And as soon as one of them got the slightest bit cut, all the others came in and sucked the blood and bit him. Most people are like turkeys. As soon as you get a little bit weak, they'll jump on you.

> J. PETER GRACE, *head of New York-based conglomerate W. R. Grace & Co., in 1976, recalling a failed boardroom attempt to oust him while he was recovering from surgery.*

My first feelings were anger. I felt betrayed. Then, I don't really know why, I thought of Gorbachev and the call he got on the meltdown at Chernobyl. This was my Chernobyl. I sat there and thought, "Why me, Lord, why me?"

> **WILLIAM SCHEYER**, *CEO of Merrill Lynch, in* Business Week *in 1987, after a bond crisis cost his firm hundreds of millions of dollars in losses.*

When down in the mouth, remember Jonah—he came out all right.

> **THOMAS EDISON**, *U.S. inventor and founder of a predecessor company to General Electric, in the late 19th century.*

Near-death experiences often reinvigorate companies. I wish Microsoft had had that opportunity. We will someday.

> **BILL GATES**, *co-founder of Microsoft, in 1996, a few years before Microsoft faced the prospect of a court-ordered breakup following a guilty verdict on antitrust charges.*

REALITY CHECK

Any idiot can face a crisis—it's this day-to-day living that wears you out.

ANTON CHEKHOV

In good times and bad your goal is always the same: to beat the competition. The smart, aggressive leader takes advantage of the slow economy and skins that guy down the road.

ROBERT CRANDALL, *former CEO of American Airlines, in 2001.*

From our beginning it has always been us, the flyweight, against the sumo wrestlers. But our years of battling with the other majors has been crucial in developing our crusader, warrior spirit.

HERB KELLEHER, *co-founder of Dallas-based Southwest Airlines, in the late 1990s. Several major carriers tried to strangle Southwest in its infancy in the 1960s and early 1970s with price wars and legal interference.*

During the rah-rah times, anybody can run a company. Anybody can hire more people, give them more money. We've had two recessions in seventeen years, and each was one year long and each was painful. But I'm glad I had those for training. They were tough times, but I think I'm a better manager for it.

T. J. RODGERS, *CEO of Cypress Semiconductor, in* Forbes ASAP *in 2001.*

The crisis was pretty critical. I wouldn't be here otherwise. The management team I put in place wouldn't be here. I used the crisis as a vehicle to get things done that wouldn't have been possible in times of business as usual.

ANNE MULCAHY, *appointed CEO of Xerox in 2001, and charged with rescuing a firm then close to bankruptcy.*

Advertising

Remember, your advertisements are in your show windows and on your counters.

> **FRANK W. WOOLWORTH**, *late-19th-century U.S. retailing magnate, on the importance of displaying merchandise attractively.*

Half my advertising is wasted, and the trouble is I don't know which half.

> **WILLIAM LEVER, LORD LEVERHULME**, *CEO of British consumer products giant Lever Bros. (now Unilever), in the early 20th century.*

Advertising is a non-moral force, like electricity, which not only illuminates, but electrocutes. Its worth to civilization depends upon how it is used.

> **J. WALTER THOMPSON**, *founder of U.S. advertising agency JWT Worldwide, in the mid-20th century.*

The faults of advertising are only those common to all human institutions. If advertising speaks to a thousand in order to influence one, so does the church. And if it encourages people to live beyond their means, so does matrimony. Good times, bad times, there will always be advertising. In good times, people want to advertise; in bad times they have to.

> **BRUCE BARTON**, *founder of U.S. advertising agency BBDO, in the mid-20th century.*

We want the consumer to say, "That's a hell of a product," instead of, "That's a hell of an ad."

LEO BURNETT, *founder of Chicago advertising agency Leo Burnett Co., creator of character-based ads featuring the Pillsbury Doughboy, the Marlboro Man, Charlie the Tuna, and the Jolly Green Giant, in the mid-20th century.*

A great ad campaign will make a bad product fail faster. It will get more people to know it's bad.

WILLIAM BERNBACH, *co-founder of U.S. advertising agency Doyle Dane Bernbach, in the mid-20th century.*

Television was not a distraction, like most peddlers; it was an attraction. The chain was not on the door when it called. The era of true mass marketing had arrived. The pitch man was no longer an interloper—he was a friend of the family.

LEONARD H. LAVIN, *founder of U.S. cosmetics firm Alberto-Culver, in an essay in* Business Decisions That Changed Our Lives (1964), *Sidney Furst and Milton Sherman, editors, on his use of TV ads.*

The armpit had its moment of glory, and the toes, with their athlete's foot.... We went through wrinkles, we went through diets.... We conquered hemorrhoids. So the businessmen sat back and said, "What's left?" And some smart guy say, "The vagina." Today the vagina, tomorrow the world.

JERRY DELLA FEMINA, *U.S. advertising agency founder, in his 1970 book* From The Wonderful Folks Who Gave You Pearl Harbor.

REALITY CHECK

> Advertising may be described as the science of arresting the human intelligence long enough to get money from it.
> **STEPHEN LEACOCK**

It doesn't matter how many people you offend, as long as you're getting your message to your consumers. I say to those people who do not want to offend anybody: You are going to have a very, very difficult time having meaningful advertising.

> **PHIL KNIGHT,** *co-founder of U.S. sportswear firm Nike, on the provocative ads with which Nike first made its mark, in the 1980s.*

I remember a man, he was such an ass. He said, "I want you to do advertising that will make all my friends at the country club come up to my table and say, 'Gee, I loved that ad of yours.'" It's a very dangerous thing, a constant temptation.

> **DAVID MACKENZIE OGILVY**, *co-founder of U.S. advertising agency Ogilvy & Mather, in* Forbes *in 1988.*

I talked about love in advertising, a word I always felt I had to decipher because businessmen acted as if love were an erotic Russian word they did not understand. (Love? What's love got to do with it?) I said that if we did not communicate that we loved our cars, nobody else would love them either. I

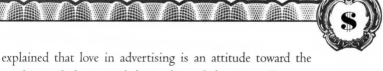

explained that love in advertising is an attitude toward the product and also toward the reader and the viewer. In some subtle way, every ad, every commercial should produce a feeling of love between the product and the potential buyer.

> MARY WELLS LAWRENCE, *co-founder of New York advertising agency Wells Rich Greene, in 2002, recalling a late 1960s meeting with executives of an ailing American Motors, which WRG helped revive.*

What consumerism really is, at worst, is getting people to buy things that don't actually improve their lives. The one thing that offends me the most is when I walk by a bank and see ads trying to convince people to take out second mortgages on their home so they can go on vacation. That's approaching evil.

> JEFF BEZOS, *founder of U.S. online retailer Amazon.com, in* Wired *in 1999.*

Ambition

I am growing old too fast.

> JAY GOULD, *19th-century U.S. railroad speculator, at age sixteen, fearful that life was passing him by.*

It's easy to work for somebody else; all you have to do is show up.

> JOHN WANAMAKER, *19th-century Philadelphia department store pioneer, on the challenge of being your own boss.*

Careful, Harry, you'll drop the world.

> **BRITON HADDEN**, *taunting Henry Luce, his partner in founding* Time *magazine in 1923, who was already exhibiting signs of grandiose ambition.*

Be Big: Think Big. Act Big. Dream Big.

> **CONRAD HILTON**, *U.S. hotelier, in his 1957 memoir,* Be My Guest.

He closed his mill at 6:00 and rested comfortably in a warm bath. I worked until 10:30 and took a cold shower in the open air, winter or summer. My business volume and profit finally surpassed my neighbor's. Once he relaxes, he will be left behind.

> **Y. C. WANG**, *Taiwanese industrialist whose stake in plastics maker Formosa Plastics Group was worth about $2.3 billion in 1987, on exploiting the complacency of a competitor.*

I never want to be the best at anything. Anybody who wants to be the best at anything in the world must spend 80 percent of their waking time on it. And you lose the pursuit of other things.

> **WARREN AVIS**, *founder of Avis Rent-A-Car, in* M *in 1987. Avis made a virtue of its runner-up status to rival Hertz, saying "When you're No. 2, you try harder."*

Everybody was writing about computers and electronics, but all I really knew about was running. It's what I've chosen to do with my life.

> **PHIL KNIGHT**, *co-founder of Nike with Bill Bowerman, his track coach at the University of Oregon, in the 1990s.*

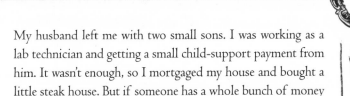

My husband left me with two small sons. I was working as a lab technician and getting a small child-support payment from him. It wasn't enough, so I mortgaged my house and bought a little steak house. But if someone has a whole bunch of money and wants to stay home with the kids, God bless 'em.

> RUTH FERTEL, *founder of Ruth's Chris Steak House, a restaurant chain based in New Orleans, in* Forbes *in 1999.*

As long as I have to lock myself in the bathroom to make phone calls like a hostage while my kids are playing in the other room, I'll question my career choices.

> STACEY SNIDER, *chairwoman of Universal Pictures, in 2000.*

Some mornings on my way into work, I see women walking along in their little tennis skirts and I wonder, "What are they doing?" For me, work is a very seductive thing. I've never wanted my life to just float by.

> HEATHER REISMAN, *CEO of Canadian bookstore chain Indigo Books, Music, and More, in 2001.*

I just wanted to be president of that thing because that's what my mother told me to do.

> KENNETH D. LEWIS, *CEO of Bank of America, in* Fortune *in 2001. On joining B of A predecessor North Carolina National Bank as a credit analyst in 1971, Lewis was asked by his mother, "How far is that from president?"*

I read with disappointment that polls report 60 percent or more of young single or married women in America prefer not to work outside the home, would choose smaller, more domestic lives…. I think young women who choose a smaller life are making a mistake. I believe that whether you are a woman or a man you are supposed to stretch everything that you are, you are supposed to love with all your might, you are supposed to have a big life, so that when all is said and done you can say to yourself, with feeling, "I loved my life so much."

> MARY WELLS LAWRENCE, *co-founder in 1966 of U.S. agency Wells Rich Greene, the first major ad agency run by a woman, in 2002.*

Autocracy

The question "Who ought to be boss?" is like asking "Who ought to tenor the quartet?" Obviously, the man who can sing tenor.

> HENRY FORD, *founder in 1903 of Ford Motor in Dearborn, Michigan.*

When I sit down, the board of directors has arrived.

> HARRY BRAKMANN HELMSLEY, *leading New York developer of the 1960s and 1970s, whose management company operated the Empire State Building and several other New York landmarks.*

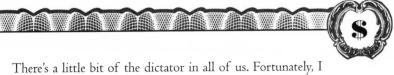

There's a little bit of the dictator in all of us. Fortunately, I was blessed with a disproportionately generous share.

> FREDRIC R. MANN, *retired chairman of National Container Corp., in the* New York Times *in 1976.*

Two people can't play the violin.

> EDWARD CROSBY (NED) JOHNSON III, *CEO of U.S. mutual funds giant Fidelity Investments, in the 1990s, justifying his autocratic management style.*

Business isn't naturally democratic. The early owner-managers were all autocrats. But leadership is a dangerous concept. We need accountability. Capitalism has really failed to achieve it.

> CHRISTOPHER HASKINS, *head of Britain's Northern Foods, in Anthony Sampson's* Company Man: The Rise and Fall of Corporate Life *(1995).*

There's too much conventionality and too little risk taking when people have to answer to one boss. You and the boss might not get along or you might spend all your time kissing the boss's ass to get ahead. You can't kiss the ass of twenty-four people. And together, those twenty-four people are more likely to have the interests of the shareholders at heart than any one person.

> JEFFREY SKILLING, *CEO of U.S. energy-trading firm Enron, in* Fortune *in 1996. At U.S. Congressional hearings after Enron's 2001 bankruptcy, subordinates testified that they were afraid to confront Skilling with their doubts about the integrity of the firm's accounting practices.*

Avarice

Greed has been severely underestimated and denigrated—unfairly so, in my opinion. There is nothing wrong with avarice as a motive, as long as it doesn't lead to dishonest or anti-social behaviour.

> **CONRAD BLACK**, *later Lord Black of Crossharbour, Anglo-Canadian press lord, in Peter C. Newman's* The Establishment Man *(1982).*

For enough money, I'd work in hell.

> **ROY THOMSON**, *later Lord Thomson of Fleet, Anglo-Canadian newspaper baron.*

You can be greedy and still feel good about yourself.

> **IVAN BOESKY**, *U.S. stock market speculator, who in the late 1980s was jailed after being convicted of engaging in illegal trading practices.*

Please don't misunderstand me. Greed is essential to the proper functioning of our economic system. Of course, we don't call it greed in polite company. On the supply side we call it hustle or ambition or push and shove. On the demand side, we call it consumerism or, playfully, "shop till you drop." But greed by any name is not something we want to eliminate. It is, after all and for better and worse, the fuel which powers the free enterprise engine.

> **WILLIAM A. DIMMA**, *head of Canadian real estate brokerage Royal LePage, in* Time *in 1989.*

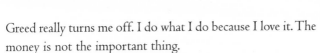

Greed really turns me off. I do what I do because I love it. The money is not the important thing.

> **HENRY KRAVIS**, *co-founder of New York-based investment banking firm Kohlberg Kravis Roberts & Co., in 1989. KKR's multibillion-dollar leveraged buyouts of the 1980s epitomized the unrestrained lusting after riches of the Reagan era.*

Greed. Greed. We all have greed. Some days you'd say, "If I could have five million dollars, I'd be the happiest person in the world." Then when you've got five, you'd want ten and there's nothing wrong with that. I mean, if it's the only thing you live for, then there's something wrong with it. But there's nothing wrong with wanting more.

> **WAYNE HUIZENGA**, *founder of the U.S. firm Blockbuster Video and owner of Florida sports teams the Miami Dolphins and the Florida Marlins, in his 1996 book* Making of a Blockbuster, *with Gail DeGeorge.*

Banking

When the panic of '93 came along, and credit was almost impossible to get, I asked the First National for some assistance, and George Baker sent me this answer: "I send you by express tonight what you asked for. If you actually need more I will take off my coat and go to work."

> **JAMES J. HILL**, *Canadian-born U.S. railroad tycoon in the 19th century, founder of the predecessor to the Burlington Northern.*

Do you work, and do you sleep well?

> **GEORGE FISHER BAKER**, *co-founder of a forerunner to Citibank and the dean of U.S. banking in the late 19th century, with a question posed to potential borrowers.*

The difference between a skinflint banker and a reckless lender is a recession.

> **WALTER WRISTON**, *the youngest person to head Citicorp when he was named president in 1967 at age forty-seven and made chairman three years later.*

A banker...[will]...go the limit of the banking laws to provide the credit you need. [But] he also has to see that you're working hard, that you're not buying fancy cars and office furniture, and that you don't take vacations.

> **MICHAEL J. CUDAHY**, *CEO of Marquette Electronics of Milwaukee, a medical equipment maker, in* Fortune *in 1984.*

I have to say that banking is the surest, safest, easiest business I have ever seen or known. If you're not actually stupid or dishonest, it's hard not to make money in banking.

> **GEORGE S. MOORE**, *head of Citibank in the 1960s, in his 1987 memoir,* The Banker's Life.

You don't discuss your banker or your gynecologist. You just trust them.

> **DIANE VON FURSTENBERG**, *U.S. apparel marketer, in 1989, asked to comment on Edmond Safra, the Geneva banker who handled her money.*

REALITY CHECK

If bankers are busy, there is something wrong.

WALTER BAGEHOT, *19th-century British economist*

Federal deposit insurance can be likened to a seductive, addictive, and deadly drug.

JOHN G. MEDLIN JR., *CEO of regional bank Wachovia of Winston-Salem, North Carolina, in 1991, on how government-insured deposits spurred many bankers to take improper risks with their depositors' funds.*

Time will tell whether I have the qualities for this job. But I've been in banking twenty-seven years, and you can teach a monkey any business after twenty-seven years. After all, it's not brain surgery.

MATTHEW W. BARRETT, *CEO of Bank of Montreal and later of Barclays, in the 1990s.*

The Wells Fargo [bank] sent a retired engineer to visit us. I spent a full afternoon with him and I have remembered ever since some advice he gave me. He said that more businesses die from indigestion than starvation. I have observed the truth of that advice many times since then.

DAVID PACKARD, *co-founder of Hewlett-Packard, in his 1995 memoir,* The HP Way: How Bill Hewlett and I Built Our Company, *on HP's philosophy of shunning costly acquisitions.*

Bankruptcy

The speaking invitations stopped coming as soon as the trouble started. That's understandable, I guess. But wouldn't you think I'd have more to tell the Canadian Club now than I did then?

> PETER MUNK, *Canadian entrepreneur, in the 1960s, on the collapse a few years earlier of Clairtone Sound, an innovative stereo equipment manufacturer whose products could be found in the living rooms of Frank Sinatra and Hugh Hefner. Munk bounced back in the 1980s and 1990s with much larger ventures in mining (Barrick Gold) and real estate (TrizecHahn).*

I really believe our ultimate competitive advantage is the fact we essentially went broke.

> THOMAS THEOBALD, *CEO of Continental Bank, who in the 1980s rebuilt the insolvent Continental Illinois Bank into a more cautious lender.*

Capitalism without bankruptcy is like Christianity without hell.

> FRANK BORMAN, *CEO of Eastern Airlines, in 1986. After sixty-three years of business, Eastern, "The Wings of Man," went bankrupt in 1991, long after Borman had left the airline.*

There is nothing like running a company that has been in Chapter 11. It's better than starting from scratch because you have rude reminders of failure all around you.

> ARNOLD HIATT, *CEO of shoe company Stride-Rite, in* Harvard Business Review *in 1992.*

Today, if I visit one of my former buildings and the elevator is not working I feel my blood pressure rise until I remember I have nothing to do with this property any more.... At Olympia & York, I was the guilty party. [But] the skills people have to build something—even if they make a mistake and lose by it—are not gone forever. I have to prove I can rebuild and re-create what has been lost by my mistakes.

> **PAUL REICHMANN**, *co-owner and chief strategist of Olympia & York Developments of Toronto, a family business and the world's largest developer prior to its 1992 collapse in the biggest bankruptcy in Canadian history, speaking in 1999. Reichmann was vindicated by the end of the decade, when O&Y's Canary Wharf office park in London—the largest European real estate project ever—filled up with the head offices of leading financial institutions.*

It's a horrible thing to see anything in its death throes. It's like a very sick person and you can't do anything about it.... It's always interesting how people approach you. They want to give you some strength, they want to help you, and they're nervous about it because they don't know how you feel, or how you're going to react. If you tell them you're fine they say: "How can you be fine if you're going through this?" And the truth is, maybe you're not really fine, but you're turning the pages. You have to go on.

> **FREDRIK STEFAN EATON**, *fourth-generation inheritor and one-time CEO of T. Eaton Co., once the largest retailer in Canada, in Canada's National Post in 1999, on the bankruptcy two years earlier of the 128-year-old Eaton's, which had sixty-three stores and seventy thousand employees when it collapsed.*

There are few things more frustrating than a director's role during bankruptcy. Much of the process is dominated and even controlled by various classes of experts representing various constituencies and plying their respective trades at what some would call extortionate rates. It is, I suppose, the inevitable ransom paid by a management and board for allowing a corporation to slip into bankruptcy in the first place.

> **WILLIAM DIMMA**, *Canadian professional corporate director, in his 2002 book* On the Board: Best Practices in Corporate Governance.

Beginnings

Bought a cheap horse, $16.... He is blind.

> **HENRY JOHN (H.J.) HEINZ**, *Pittsburgh food magnate, in a diary notation at about the time his first business, a horseradish processor, was forced into bankruptcy during the nationwide financial panic of 1875.*

I am myself lamentably ignorant. The competition in the business world is such that the people with good educations are usually those who succeed.

> **WILLIAM KEITH KELLOGG**, *founder in 1906 of cereal giant Kellogg Co., in a letter to his son. W. K. Kellogg left school at thirteen, branded a slow learner by his parents and teachers.*

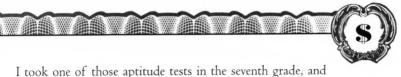

I took one of those aptitude tests in the seventh grade, and they said, "You're not much good at anything, so why don't you go into business?"

> **J. WILLARD (BILL) MARRIOTT JR.**, *CEO of U.S. hotelier Marriott International, founded by his father in 1929.*

I found I didn't want to take care of sick people. I wanted to help people keep their health and beauty.

> **ELIZABETH ARDEN**, *Canadian-born U.S. cosmetics entrepreneur, a rival to Revlon and Estée Lauder at the height of her fortunes, in the 1950s. Born Florence Nightingale Graham, she felt obliged to try nursing, but gave it up after just three weeks.*

I'll tell you the worst. I am a college graduate and the son of a minister. But I mean to pay.

> **ARTHUR VINING DAVIS**, *founder of Alcoa, seeking a $200 grubstake for his aluminum business from Pittsburgh financier Andrew W. Mellon. Prior to the mid-20th century, successful tycoons were rarely drawn from the ranks of academe, and religious leaders were often known to doubt the moral bearing of those in headlong pursuit of commercial gain.*

My eyes fell on two posters. The top poster announced a Battle of the Bands between Stan Kenton and Duke Ellington. The one below was advertising a bout between two young fighters. I stared at both posters for some time, realizing the fighters could fight once and maybe not fight again for three or four weeks, or months, or never. The bands were

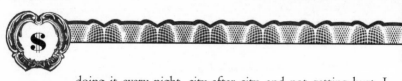

doing it every night, city after city, and not getting hurt. I then noticed the fighters were about twenty-three and looked fifty; the band leaders about fifty and looked twenty-three.

> **BERRY GORDY**, *founder of Motown Records, on the 1950 epiphany that prompted him to give up his career as a pro boxer and go into the music business.*

I, who would one day affect the destiny of the nation, was cleaning crap.

> **TED TURNER**, *U.S. media mogul who inherited his father's debt-ridden billboard company in 1963 and founded pioneering cable news network CNN in 1980, recalling his latrine and other menial duties during a brief stint in the U.S. Coast Guard.*

Tell him, Mom! Tell him it worked last night!

> **BILL GATES**, *future co-founder of Microsoft, turning for help to his mother, Mary Gates, in the early 1970s, when the teenaged programmer's Traf-O-Data system that was to log traffic for the city of Bellevue, Washington, crashed during an early sales pitch to the prospective client.*

I decided law was the exact opposite of sex: even when it was good it was lousy.

> **MORTIMER ZUCKERMAN**, *graduate in law from McGill University, in the 1980s, on why he opted for a career in real estate and publishing as owner of the* New York Daily News, U.S.News & World Report *and* Atlantic Monthly.

I'm not going to sell my name.

> **JOHN E. SWEARINGEN**, *recently retired CEO of U.S. oil giant Standard Oil (Indiana), later Amoco, telling the* Wall Street Journal *in the early 1980s that he would not be launching a second career as a professional director.*

REALITY CHECK

Went to the yearly court of the Edinburgh Assurance Co., to which I am one of those graceful and useless appendages called "Directors Extraordinary."

> **SIR WALTER SCOTT**, *diary notation in 1825.*

Strategies are okayed in boardrooms that even a child would say are bound to fail. The problem is there is never a child in the boardroom.

> **VICTOR H. PALMIERI**, *turnaround CEO at a succession of troubled U.S. firms, in the 1980s.*

You can't build a strong corporation with a lot of committees and a board that has to be consulted at every turn. You have to be able to make decisions on your own.

> **RUPERT MURDOCH**, *Australian American media baron, in the 1990s.*

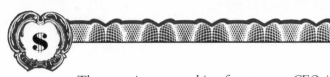

The most important thing for any new CEO is to have a board that makes you look ten feet tall with hair, that works full time telling you how good you are, how smart you are.

> JACK WELCH, *CEO of General Electric, in the 1990s.*

Bluntly stated, a "woman's view" on how to run our semi-conductor company does not help us, unless that woman has an advanced technical degree and experience as a CEO... You ought to get down from your moral high horse.

> T. J. RODGERS, *CEO of California-based Cypress Semiconductor, responding to a nun who called on him to make his board more diverse, reported in the* Wall Street Journal *in 1996.*

Celebrity

The whale only gets harpooned when he spouts.

> HENRY LEA HILLMAN, *press-shy Pittsburgh industrialist and inheritor of his father's Pittsburgh Coke & Chemical, in 1959.*

I envy Iacocca. If they asked me, I'd do a *Miami Vice* episode; I'd even do *Hill Street Blues.* Having a high profile is a positive thing if it stimulates people to look into the company.

> W. JEREMIAH SANDERS III, *founder of Advanced Micro Devices, in 1986, after Chrysler turnaround CEO Lee Iacocca made a guest appearance on* Miami Vice, *a popular TV police drama.*

People like symbols, and in looking for a symbol for Apple, many times they latched on to me. Other competitors were fairly impersonal, organizational entities, whereas Apple was in many ways like a person in formation, like somebody growing up.

    STEVE JOBS, *co-founder of Apple Computer, who became nearly synonymous with the company, in* Business Week *in 1986.*

It's a two-edged sword. It lengthens my day. I don't have a minute to myself. But I worked for twenty-seven or twenty-eight years in anonymity. All of a sudden, when you get recognition, there's a glow.

    VICTOR KIAM, *CEO of U.S. shaving products company Remington, in* Business Week *in 1986, after appearing in television ads for Remington shavers.*

If I go to make a courtesy call on the king or crown prince of Saudi Arabia, we don't particularly discuss banking business. But everyone down the line knows I've seen them, so my ability to get things done is clearly advanced by the fact that I have been to see the king.

    DAVID ROCKEFELLER, *CEO of Chase Manhattan Bank, in the 1980s.*

I was made a hero and then, when exaggerated expectations were not totally fulfilled, I was heavily criticized. You have people who think you can solve all the problems or that you're to blame for everything that doesn't work. That's not realistic in organizations with tens of thousands of people.

> **DR. DANIEL VASELLA**, *CEO of Swiss pharmaceuticals group Novartis, in the* Financial Times *in 2001, criticizing the cult status of CEOs in the 1990s.*

It's got to stop. I told my assistant Irene the other day that we have to make a rule. No more autographs, no more celebrity stuff. I said to her, "You are just going to have to say 'he doesn't live here anymore', or 'he died.'" I want to simplify my life.

> **LEE IACOCCA**, *former CEO of Chrysler and credited with rescuing the automaker in the 1980s, at age seventy-one, in an interview in* Fortune *in 1996.*

This man does fascinate me. I have high respect for what he has achieved, and for his undoubted intuition. But sometimes when I see that bearded face in (yet another) facile photo opportunity, I reflect that, sometimes, there just isn't enough vomit in the world.

> **BARRY J. GIBBONS**, *CEO of U.S. fast-food chain Burger King in the early 1990s, in his 2002 book* Dream Merchants & Howboys: Mavericks, Nutters, and the Road to Business Success, *discussing fellow British businessman Sir Richard Branson.*

Communication

I cannot overemphasize the importance of getting out of your office and listening to what the employees are saying. You listen for that quiet panic that can develop when some operation—or some individual—is not doing as well as the official reports would indicate.

> RICHARD M. FURLAUD, *chairman of U.S. pharmaceutical maker Pfizer, in* Fortune *in 1975.*

Do not summon people to your office—it frightens them. Instead go to see them in *their* offices. This makes you visible throughout the agency. A chairman who never wanders about his agency becomes a hermit, out of touch with his staff.

> DAVID MACKENZIE OGILVY, *co-founder in 1949 of U.S. advertising agency Ogilvy & Mather.*

If you've got a problem, share it. Then we all have a problem. If you don't, and it grows, it's your ass.

> JOHN B. McCOY, *CEO of Bank One of Columbus, Ohio, transformed by McCoy in the 1980s into one of the largest U.S. regional banks, in the 1990s.*

Once you let people in your office, they'll come in and out all day long. I need to think.

> PHIL KNIGHT, *co-founder of shoe maker Nike and no fan of "open-door" policies, in the 1990s.*

The phone has become a symbol of non-communication because people are never in their offices.

> **JAY CHIAT**, *chairman of U.S. advertising agency Chiat/Day, whose new Los Angeles offices were equipped with cellular phones and a computer network rather than fixed desks and filing cabinets, in the 1990s.*

If someone isn't saying something of interest, it's easier not to respond to their mail than it is not to answer the phone.

> **BILL GATES**, *co-founder of Microsoft, cited in Anthony Sampson's,* Company Man: The Rise and Fall of Corporate Life *(1995). Gates shunned the phone, but was a prolific email correspondent.*

Too many company people are intimidated by the guy or the woman who's the CEO, who hovers above reality, remote, detached and inhuman. I sort of lay out all my imperfections. Yes, my hair is thinning and my waist is thickening!

> **MATTHEW W. BARRETT**, *CEO of Barclays, Britain's largest bank, in a London* Sunday Telegraph *interview in 2002. At Barclays, Barrett held dozens of meetings with rank-and-file employees. Many of them were curious about the trophy wife who dumped Barrett, news of which appeared in British tabloids when Barrett's appointment at Barclays was first announced.*

Anybody who proclaims an "open door" policy is a lousy manager. The statement itself changes interaction by suggesting employees come to the manager, instead of the manager going to the employees. One thing Dave Packard [co-founder of Hewlett-Packard] did was constantly patrol the building, finding out what was going on. He never needed an "open door" since he was never inside his cubicle anyway.

> **GARY SUTTON**, *CEO of several U.S. firms in the 1980s and 1990s, in the* Wall Street Journal *in 2002.*

Compensation, Employee

The root of existing trouble lies in the fact that the employee takes no interest in his work and has no consideration for his employer's property or welfare.

> **WILLIAM COOPER PROCTER**, *grandson of the co-founder of Procter & Gamble, on the rationale for what is believed to be the first profit-sharing plan at a major U.S. company, in 1887.*

You can do a lot of talking to your employees, and you can buy turkeys at Christmas if that's your hobby. But what's going to make the employee happy is what's in the pay envelope at the end of every week when he shakes it. And then the benefit plans.

> **THOMAS J. WATSON SR.**, *founder of the modern IBM, in the mid-20th century.*

People will always work harder if they're getting well paid. If you pay peanuts, you get monkeys.

> **ARMAND HAMMER**, *CEO of U.S.-based Occidental Petroleum in the 1980s.*

REALITY CHECK

There's no praise to beat the sort you can put in your pocket.
  MOLIÈRE

The most visible sign of the open corporation at Next is our policy of allowing everybody to know what salary everybody else is making. There's a list in the finance department, and anyone can go look at it.

> **STEVE JOBS**, *co-founder of Apple Computer and founder of software firm Next, in the 1980s. The short-lived pay-disclosure scheme was widely ridiculed in Silicon Valley.*

The day I'm laid out dead with an apple in my mouth is the day we'll pay commissions. If you pay commissions, you imply that the small customer isn't worth anything.

> **BERNARD MARCUS**, *co-founder of U.S. retailer Home Depot, in* Fortune *in 1993.*

The best way to relieve a critical recruiting situation is to raise pay. You can say we're going to give you a pension plan or twenty cents more an hour, and it's the twenty cents that's going to grab them.

> **MITCHELL FROMSTEIN**, *CEO of U.S. employment agency Manpower, in the* Wall Street Journal *in 1996.*

Compensation, Executive

Money itch is a bad thing. I never had that trouble.

> **A. P. GIANNINI**, *founder in 1904 of Bank of America and a pioneer in popularizing financial services among savers of modest income. For years Giannini accepted virtually no salary, and when his board once surprised him with a $1.5 million bonus, Giannini promptly gave all of it to the University of California.*

That's the American way. If little kids don't aspire to make money like I did, what the hell good is this country?

> **LEE IACOCCA**, *CEO of Chrysler, in 1987, justifying his $20.6 million in annual compensation at a time when Chrysler was cutting employee merit pay.*

When I look at overpaid executives I feel like a New England Protestant minister watching Jimmy Swaggart on TV.

> **T. J. RODGERS**, *CEO of Cypress Semiconductor of San Jose, California, in 1991. His own compensation of $250,000 in 1990 was near the bottom for his industry.*

The Steve Rosses of the world are brilliant. It's a big bear they handle, and if they handle the big bear successfully, I think they should get a big bear of a reward.

> **LINDA WACHNER**, *CEO of U.S. lingerie maker Warnaco, in* Forbes *in 1991. Steve Ross received stupendous compensation after merging his Warner Communications—a company with a track record of mediocre earnings—with Time Inc. in 1989.*

America is still a kind of frontier society which respects the richest man in town.

> **SIR OWEN GREEN**, *CEO of British conglomerate BTR, in Anthony Sampson's,* Company Man: The Rise and Fall of Corporate Life *(1995), recalling the reply he got upon asking one of his American directors why he sought such a large salary: "It's the score."*

I think executive compensation should in some way be related to sustained profit growth. Anybody can hit the ball out of the park once. The trick is to hit it out of the park fifty times a year for ten years in a row.

> **RICHARD (DICK) CURRIE**, *in the* Financial Post *in 2001. In a twenty-five-year career at Canadian supermarket chain Loblaws, ending in 2000, Currie boosted the firm's market capitalization from $40 million to $14 billion (Cdn).*

A chief executive who milks a company with excessive salary, bonus, options, pensions, and expenses (for aircraft, trips, etc.), is not a professional. How can he or she have the respect of subordinates? How can he ask them to set an example to impose tight controls when he operates from greed?

> **STEPHEN JARISLOWSKY**, *CEO of Jarislowsky Fraser Ltd., an investment management firm with $29 billion (Cdn.) in assets, in Canada's* National Post *in 2002, on the recent trend of failed CEOs at Enron, Global Crossing, Nortel Networks, and other firms enriching themselves with proceeds from extravagant compensation packages approved by their boards.*

Competing

It's like trying to screw an elephant.

> **HENRY FORD**, *founder in 1903 of Ford Motor, on trying to compete with the larger General Motors.*

Never try to take a fortified hill, especially if the army on top is bigger than your own.

> **WILLIAM (BILL) HEWETT**, *co-founder in 1939 of Hewlett-Packard, which avoided direct competition with IBM.*

I never look at the competition—I don't even know who the competition is: Every day they have a different president.

> **ESTÉE LAUDER**, *U.S. cosmetics entrepreneur who founded Estée Lauder Inc. in 1946, on the revolving door at rival Revlon.*

What do you do when your competitor's drowning? Get a live hose and stick it in his mouth.

> **RAY KROC**, *founder of McDonald's, in the 1970s. The mantra was later adopted by Douglas Ivester, briefly CEO of Coca-Cola in the late 1990s.*

Make money, a lot of it, and be most injurious to the competition.

> **FRED W. SMITH**, *founder in 1973 of Memphis-based FedEx.*

We never look at our competitors' products. Why should we assume they know what they're doing? We push our managers to be creative, challenge them not to beat the competition, but to rewrite the rules.

> **MICHAEL BLOOMBERG**, *founder in the 1980s of U.S. information services firm Bloomberg.*

I do not think it is possible to fight tanks with cavalry. [Apple Computer co-founder] Steve Jobs challenging IBM was like watching the Poles try to resist the Nazis in the last World War.

> **CARLO DE BENEDETTI**, *CEO of Italian technology firm Olivetti, in 1985.*

I may be over the top on this, but I just don't want to like my competitors. I want my people to believe that whenever he and our other competitors succeed, we will be less able to do all the things we want to do.

> **PHIL KNIGHT**, *co-founder of U.S. sportswear firm Nike, on his rival Paul Fireman, CEO of Reebok, in the 1990s. Of Knight, Fireman said, "At the end of the contest, I'd shake hands and walk away. I think he would throw a shovel of dirt on the grave."*

We don't have competitors. We bought most of the competitors.

> **GORDON EUBANKS JR.**, *CEO of network software firm Symantec, on his strategy for dealing with rivals, in the 1990s.*

Mommy...Daddy...Daddy, kill Compaq. Daddy, kill IBM. Daddy, kill Gateway.

> **MICHAEL S. DELL**, *founder of U.S. computer maker Dell Computer, quoted in 1995 from a pep talk to employees in which he joked about his daughter's first words.*

I don't like our competitors. I don't eat with them, don't do anything with them except try to waste them.

> **HUGH MCCOLL**, *CEO of Nationsbank, in the* Wall Street Journal *in 1996.*

This is not warfare. I don't consider our competitors as Communists or Hitler.

> **EMMANUEL A. KAMPOURIS**, *CEO of American Standard, a U.S. maker of bathroom fixtures, in* Business Week *in 1996.*

They hate me because I compete and I enjoy competing. I like to get my teeth into their flesh. I rip their flesh right off the bone.

> **TERRY MATTHEWS**, *founder of Newbridge Networks of Kanata, Ontario, in 1998, on why his rivals dislike him.*

How much do we need to pay you to screw Netscape?

> **BILL GATES**, *CEO of Microsoft, to an America Online executive in an internal email message that surfaced in the U.S. Justice Department's late-1990s antitrust suit against Microsoft.*

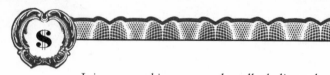

It is a war, and in wars people really do live and people do die.

> LESLIE WEXNER, *founder and CEO of U.S. retailer The Limited, in* WAR (Winning at Retail), *a motivational video for managers, in 1999.*

I want you to go back charged up to squash *Glamour*, completely obliterate them, make them like a little armadillo on the road.

> CATHARINE P. BLACK, *president of Hearst Magazines, in 2002 to a gathering of editors of international editions of* Cosmopolitan, *a Hearst title, which faced new competition abroad from foreign editions of the rival Condé Nast magazine* Glamour.

Consultants

If ever I wanted to kill opposition [rivals] by unfair means I would endow the opposition with experts. They would have so much good advice that I could be sure they would do little work.

> HENRY FORD, *founder in 1903 of Ford Motor in Dearborn, Michigan.*

REALITY CHECK

In the multitude of counselors, there is safety.

> PROVERBS *11:14*

A consultant is an individual handsomely paid for telling senior management of problems about which senior management's own employees have told the consultant. The consultant thus offers the advantage of generally having had no firsthand experience in the matters of interest, thereby assuring a clear mind uncluttered by any of the facts.

> NORMAN R. AUGUSTINE, *CEO of U.S. defense contractor Lockheed Martin, in his 1986 book,* Augustine's Laws.

As for the corporate consultants who advise [boards of directors] on salary, all I can say is that prostitution would be a step up for them.

> CHARLES T. (CHARLIE) MUNGER, *vice-chairman of U.S. investment firm Berkshire Hathaway, in the late 1990s.*

I was increasingly baffled about the whole consultation process, which seemed to be little more than McKinsey's regurgitating what we had told them in a slightly different, but not very helpful way.

> KATHARINE GRAHAM, *CEO of Washington Post Co., in her 1997 memoir,* Personal History. *Graham recalled McKinsey & Co.'s advice to Graham not to repurchase shares in her own company, which it regarded as fully priced, but which later skyrocketed. "Don [Graham's son and successor as CEO] referred to the page in McKinsey's report on which the suggestion was made as the 'half-billion-dollar page,' given that's what it probably cost us in lost value to the company," Graham wrote.*

Contrarian

A pioneer is a guy with an arrow in his back and his face in the mud.

> **J. WILLARD (BILL) MARRIOTT SR.**, *U.S. hotelier who paid his college tuition by selling underwear and who, with wife Alice, opened his first nine-seat root beer stand in 1927 in Washington, D.C.*

People contended that the wiener didn't merit that kind of treatment. But it did.

> **OSCAR M. MAYER**, *who conceived the first brand-name hot dog in the 1930s.*

No one can possibly achieve any real and lasting success or get rich in business by being a conformist.

> **J. PAUL GETTY**, *U.S. oilman, in the* International Herald Tribune *in 1961.*

A touch of craziness.... Crazy people see and feel things that others don't. An entrepreneur's dream is often a kind of madness.

> **ANITA RODDICK**, *co-founder in 1976 of cosmetics retailer Body Shop International.*

REALITY CHECK

The cleverly expressed opposite of any generally accepted idea is worth a fortune to somebody.

F. Scott Fitzgerald

We should do something when people say it is crazy. If people say something is good, it means that someone else is already doing it.

Hajime Mitarai, *president of Canon, a leading Japanese camera maker that became a serious rival to Xerox in photocopiers in the 1980s.*

We were the children of Holden Caufield. Nobody liked the phoniness or the hypocrisy of the establishment, including the business establishment.

Phil Knight, *co-founder of Nike, in the 1990s, on the mindset of his generation of entrepreneurs. The reference is to the protagonist in J. D. Salinger's* The Catcher in the Rye.

There's a lot of comfort in being with similarly disturbed people.

Robert Iverson, *founder of Kiwi International Airlines, in* Inc. *in 1994, on why he launched a business in an industry with a high casualty rate.*

Corporate Culture

It is not necessary for people to love each other in order to work together. Too much good fellowship may indeed be very bad for it may lead to one man trying to cover up the faults of another.

> HENRY FORD, *founder in 1903 of Ford Motor in Dearborn, Michigan.*

Microsoft expects a level of dedication from its employees higher than most companies. Therefore, if some deadline or discussion or interesting piece of work causes you to work extra time some week it just goes with the job.

> BILL GATES, *co-founder of Microsoft, in a memo from the company's early days in the 1970s.*

I don't really give a damn about a white shirt, but if I wear a nice-looking blue shirt, the next fellow down is going to wear a purple shirt, and then...we're going to have an aloha shirt down at the salesman level.

> THOMAS J. WATSON JR., *CEO of IBM, in the late 1980s, on the company's famously strict dress code.*

I'm almost trying not to understand IBM's culture.

> LOUIS V. GERSTNER JR., *CEO of IBM, in* Fortune *in 1993, soon after he began his successful effort to turn around the sclerotic computer giant.*

Our dress code is, you must dress.

> SCOTT MCNEALY, *CEO of California-based computer firm Sun Microsystems, in the late 1990s.*

You want to have an organization that is humble and proud, that is confident but not arrogant, is confident but not self-delusional.... If we had everybody saying we're not arrogant, my guess is we would be servile.

> HARVEY GOLUB, *CEO of American Express, in* Fortune *in 1995.*

Apple has to be more pragmatic and less religious. And the only one who can really do that is the person who created the religion in the first place [Apple co-founder Steve Jobs].

> JOHN SCULLEY, *former CEO of Apple Computer, in* Newsweek *in 1997. Jobs, ousted from Apple in favor of Sculley, did return as CEO in the late 1990s and Apple enjoyed a revival in its fortunes.*

I'm not blending any cultures. I'm acquiring you.... Look at your paycheck next month. I bet it says CA at the top left-hand corner.

> CHARLES WANG, *CEO of Computer Associates, in a 1997 memo to employees of a recently acquired company.*

It's the intangibles that are the hardest things for a competitor to imitate. You can get an airplane. You can get ticket-counter space; you can get baggage conveyors. But it is our

esprit de corps—the culture, the spirit—that is truly our most valuable competitive asset.

> **HERB KELLEHER**, *co-founder of Dallas-based Southwest Airlines, in* Time *in 1999.*

A big part of our culture is storytelling. People sit down in the cafeteria and one person asks another, "What's it really like to work here?" And one of the things they talk about is whether we stood on our principles of fair treatment in forcing out people as high as general managers and vice-presidents who were abusing the employees' trust.

> **ISADORE SHARP**, *CEO of Toronto-based Four Seasons Hotels, in 2000. In a managerial shakeup in the 1990s, Sharp fired some top managers who he believed, on the basis of employee feedback, were too self-aggrandizing to be effective team players.*

Corporate Finance

By last year we were wreaking havoc everywhere. Everything we touched turned to gold. Hell, we even took our mistakes public! The investment bankers were our partners in crime. Did we know it couldn't last? Of course! We were sure we could form a company, get it up and running, and then sell it to another overvalued company before reality set in. We raised bigger and bigger venture funds, and we told our entrepreneurs to "go big or go home!" The fools—they believed us.

> HOWARD ANDERSON, *founder of the Yankee Group and YankeeTek Ventures, a venture capital firm in Cambridge, Massachusetts, in* Forbes ASAP *on the dot-com implosion of 2000–2001.*

Financing is the art of passing currency from hand to hand until it finally disappears.

> ROBERT W. SARNOFF, *founder of RCA, in the mid-20th century.*

When you cut out the investment bankers, you usually cut out the leaks.

> T. BOONE PICKENS, *corporate raider and CEO of Mesa Petroleum, in* Fortune *in 1987.*

We've been shaky since Day One. The minute we cease to be undercapitalized, I'll know we've got too much money.

> LEONARD RIGGIO, *CEO of Barnes & Noble, in 1976. Riggio started with an off-campus bookstore near New York University, launched with a grubstake of $10,000 in borrowed funds.*

I sat through board meeting after board meeting not knowing the difference between net and gross and really struggling. And then, finally, last year somebody said to me, "Now look, Richard, we know you're never quite sure whether it's good news or bad news when we give you the figures, but think of the Atlantic and think of the fish all over the ocean. If you've got fish in the net that's what you've caught—all the rest is gross." I thought, fantastic. I've finally got there.

> SIR RICHARD BRANSON, *CEO of British conglomerate Virgin Group, cited in* EuroMoney *magazine in 2001. Branson, who suffers from dyslexia, explained in* Fortune *in 2002 that his staffers used simple metaphors to help him grasp arcane concepts in corporate finance.*

Customer Satisfaction

No sale is really complete until the product is worn out, and the customer is satisfied.

> L. L. (LEON LEONWOOD) BEAN, *founder in 1912 of U.S. catalog retailer L.L. Bean, based in Freeport, Maine, who borrowed money to make good on his first money-back offer on the sale of one hundred hybrid hunting boots, ninety of which fell apart.*

Some examples of customer dissatisfaction were of the most drastic sort: four healthy, husky—and irate—longshoremen heaving a recalcitrant beverage machine off a pier and into the ocean; three burly customers hurling a large beverage machine into an open hearth furnace at a steel mill.

> DAVRE J. DAVIDSON AND WILLIAM S. FISHMAN, *co-founders of U.S. vending-machine operator ARA Service (Automatic Retailers of America), in an essay, "Serving People—Where They Are" in* Business Decisions That Changed Our Lives *(1964).*

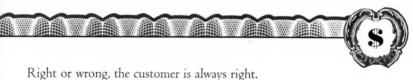

Right or wrong, the customer is always right.

> **MARSHALL FIELD**, *19th-century Chicago department store merchant who gained fame with his motto, "Give the lady what she wants."*

Our customers are not there to field-test our products.

> **STANLEY GAULT**, *CEO of U.S. household products company Rubbermaid, in* Time *in 1989.*

I believe the new trends include the requirement on the part of the customer that the vehicle will work.

> **SIR GRAHAM DAY**, *incoming CEO of British automaker Rover Group, whose products were plagued with defects, in 1990.*

If you really listen to your customers, they're never happy—they'll let you know what you're doing wrong. Fat headedness is what bothers me most. I think we get so much press about our good service and we start believing it, and then we think we're better than the customer. And then we're dead.

> **BRUCE NORDSTROM**, *co-chairman of Nordstrom, a leading U.S. department store retailer, in a 1991 interview in* The Reporter, *a publication of the business school at Stanford University.*

You don't hear about GE's manufacturing problems. My barber looks at me like I murdered my mother.

> **ANDREW S. GROVE**, *CEO of Intel, the world's largest maker of semiconductors, in* Fortune *in 1997, recalling the criticism he suffered a few years earlier over glitches in a newly launched super-chip.*

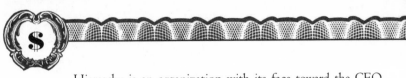

Hierarchy is an organization with its face toward the CEO, and its ass toward the customer. Pleasing the boss should never be more important than pleasing the customer.

> JACK WELCH, *CEO of General Electric, in the early 1990s.*

We do not talk to any End Users.

> BILL GATES, *co-founder of Microsoft, which gained a near monopoly in PC operating-system software, in the early 1980s.*

Working with users will help us respond to their needs.

> AN WANG, *founder of customer-friendly computer maker Wang Laboratories of Massachusetts, which collapsed in the late 1980s.*

I asked a psychologist recently why he thought people react so violently to service charges, and he said maybe they're feeling like somebody who has just been charged for breakfast by their mother.

> MATTHEW W. BARRETT, *CEO of Bank of Montreal and later of Barclays, in* Heidrick & Struggles International Leadership Journal *in 1997.*

I once read a single sentence by a company president that sums up success. "The most important marketer in our company is the man or woman who decides not to drop the box in the back of the delivery truck."

> ISADORE SHARP, *founder of Toronto-based Four Seasons Hotels, in 2000.*

The danger with a drug like Xenical is that people take it three weeks before they go to the beach and expect results that the drug can't deliver. You need to get the right patients.

> **FRANZ HUBER**, *CEO of Swiss drugmaker Roche, in 2001, responding to criticism that Xenical, the firm's anti-obesity drug, was ineffective.*

If your watch stopped every other day, would you wear it? You would throw it away. It's of no value to you. We cannot be good one day and lousy the next.

> **GORDON BETHUNE**, *CEO of Houston-based Continental Airlines, in 2001.*

Customer Service

We can rebuild the plant, but we may never get back the lost goodwill.

> **OWEN D. YOUNG**, *CEO of General Electric from 1922 to 1939, instructing his managers that if they were feeling grumpy they should blow up a plant before barking at a customer.*

Service is not a kind of blackmail paid to representatives of social morality; it is the way money is made. Service is what the typical American businessman would do his best to render even if there weren't a cop or a preacher in sight.

> **HENRY LUCE**, *co-founder of Time Inc., in a 1950* Fortune *essay.*

Now, I want you to raise your right hand—and remember what we say at Wal-Mart, that a promise we make is a promise we keep—and I want you to repeat after me: From this day forward, I solemnly promise and declare that every time a customer comes within ten feet of me, I will smile, look him in the eye, and greet him. So help me Sam.

> **SAM WALTON**, *founder and CEO of Wal-Mart Stores, instruction to employees in the mid-1980s. In his 1992 autobiography,* Made in America, *Walton complained that store employees seldom observed his "ten-foot" rule.*

People are so unaccustomed to very good service that when they see it they are dazzled by it.

> **JAMES BARKSDALE**, *CEO of Federal Express and later of Netscape Communications, in* U.S. News & World Report *in 1984.*

One of my senior flight attendants, an old and conscientious pro, put it this way: "Sir, the trouble is that the passengers don't meet *our* standards anymore."

> **ROBERT L. CRANDALL**, *CEO of American Airlines, in 1988, on how cut-throat pricing after industry deregulation was attracting a different class of customers.*

REALITY CHECK

We don't have to care. We're the phone company.
LILY TOMLIN

The customer doesn't expect everything will go right all the time; the big test is what you do when things go wrong.

> SIR COLIN MARSHALL, *chairman of British Airways, in* Harvard Business Review *in 1995.*

Everybody says they provide great service these days, and except for Nordstrom and Ritz-Carlton and a few others, they are all full of shit. Self-service, when provided properly, is the best kind of service there is.

> JIM SINEGAL, *CEO of U.S. discount retailer Price Costco, in* Fortune *in 1995.*

Debt

Balance sheets reveal the past; this loan is for the future.

> THOMAS J. WATSON SR., *founder of the modern IBM, which he joined in 1914 when it was the Computing-Tabulating-Recording Co., responding to bankers who fretted over IBM's fragile finances when he asked for their support to fund a new research division.*

It's not what you have but how much you can borrow that's important in business.

> WALT DISNEY, *CEO of Burbank, California-based Walt Disney Co., which he co-founded in 1923.*

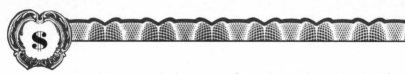

Don't borrow a little money. If you do, you have a lender. If you borrow a lot, you have a partner.

> **FRED W. SMITH**, *founder of Memphis-based Federal Express in 1973.*

Dad said, "Never borrow money unless you can get it paid back." I guess I didn't listen well enough.

> **WILLIAM HERBERT HUNT**, *who, with brother Bunker Hunt—children of Texas oilman H.L. Hunt—carried a huge debt to cover a failed $1.1 billion scheme to corner the world silver market in 1980.*

You don't deserve to be called an entrepreneur unless you've mortgaged your house to the business.

> **EDWARD S. (TED) ROGERS**, *Canadian cable-TV mogul, in 1985.*

REALITY CHECK

Business? It's quite simple. It's other people's money.

> **ALEXANDRE DUMAS THE YOUNGER**

Leverage was the beverage
that got this party cookin';
but the hangover's set in,
and now a Gravedancer's lookin'.

> **SAM ZELL**, *Chicago real estate developer and sometime writer of bad poetry with an estimated net worth of $425 million in 1992, whose nickname—derived from his skill at profiting from distressed properties—was "the grave dancer."*

Decisions

After a certain key point you must move ahead as if a project were assured—in order to assure it—because if you wait around for all the pieces of the puzzle to fit before closing a deal, you can wait forever.

> **WILLIAM ZECKENDORF,** *U.S. real estate developer, whose projects included Washington's l'Enfant Plaza, Denver's Mile High Center and Montreal's Place Ville Marie, and whose firm, Webb & Knapp, spiraled into bankruptcy in 1965, in his 1970 memoir,* Zeckendorf.

Judgment comes from experience—and experience comes from bad judgment.

> **WALTER WRISTON,** *CEO of Citicorp, in the 1980s.*

Nothing is worse than procrastination. When I look at ten decisions I regret or failed to make, there will be nine of them where I delayed.

> **PERCY BARNEVIK,** *CEO of Swedish-Swiss engineering firm ABB, in the* New York Times *in 1990.*

I think it's unfortunate that to some degree the word "entrepreneur" has taken on the connotation of a gambler. Many times action is not the most risky path. The most risky path is inaction.

> **FRED W. SMITH,** *founder of Memphis-based Federal Express in 1973.*

"A bad decision on Monday is better than a good one on Friday." What bedevils our business is lack of speedy response.

> SIR MARTIN SORRELL, *CEO of WPP, a London-based advertising group, in Jeffrey E. Garten,* The Mind of the C.E.O. *(2001).*

When you are faced with a decision, the best thing is to do the right thing, the next best is to do the wrong thing, and the worst is to do nothing.

> ROGER A. ENRICO, *CEO of U.S. soft-drink maker PepsiCo, in 2000.*

Delegating

Has anyone given you the law of these offices? No? It is this: Nobody does anything if he can get anybody else to do it. As soon as you can, get someone whom you can rely on, train him in the work, sit down, cock up your heels, and think out some way for Standard Oil to make some money.

> JOHN D. ROCKEFELLER SR., *founder of U.S. company Standard Oil, in the late 19th century.*

How could you let me do this to myself?

> CHARLES REVSON, *co-founder of U.S. cosmetics giant Revlon, reprimanding a subordinate for failing to dissuade him from a poor decision. Cited in Andrew Tobias's,* Fire and Ice: The Story of Charles Revson—the Man Who Built the Revlon Empire *(1975).*

The length of the rope may vary, but there must be rope.

ROBERT C. WILSON, *CEO of U.S. computer equipment maker Memorex, in* Fortune *in 1976, on the need to grant autonomy to subordinates.*

REALITY CHECK

If you want a thing done, go—if not, send.

BENJAMIN FRANKLIN

Whatever power I exert is collegial.

KATHARINE GRAHAM, *CEO of the* Washington Post, *which she ran from 1963, after the death of her husband, the paper's publisher, until the early 1990s.*

The real problem is that execution just doesn't sound sexy. It's the stuff a leader delegates. Do great CEOs and Nobel Prize winners achieve their glory through execution?

LARRY BOSSIDY, *CEO of Honeywell and former CEO of AlliedSignal, in 2002, on the tendency of CEOs to delegate hiring top people to human resources departments and formulating strategy to strategic development teams—who produce reports that gather dust, or "credenza ware," as he called them. "There are a lot of different leadership styles, but these hands-off CEOs—I just don't get it," said Bossidy.*

Divesting

It is generally considered more comfortable to take a dog's tail off all at once rather than an inch at a time.

> CHARLES L. BROWN, *CEO of AT&T, in 1983, rationalizing his decision to sell or close several businesses and suffer a $5.2 billion write-off.*

Almost everything I have is for sale, except my kids and possibly my wife.

> CARL ICAHN, *U.S. financier and controlling shareholder in airline TWA in the 1990s, in 1984.*

If you can't fix it, sell it. If you can't sell it, shoot it.

> ALLEN BORN, *CEO of U.S. mining firm Amax, in the 1980s.*

If it makes money, we expand it. If it doesn't, we cut its throat.

> DON TYSON, *head of Arkansas poultry giant Tyson Foods, in the 1990s.*

Sometimes I've stayed too long with people when I should have moved on sooner, or with an investment that I should have corrected quicker. Sometimes strong people think they can change almost anything, and sometimes it's better just to come to grips with a problem and resolve it.

> LODWRICK M. COOK, *CEO of Atlantic Richfield, in* Forbes *in 1988.*

Gin rummy managerial behavior (discard your least promising business at each turn) is not our style.

> **WARREN BUFFETT,** *CEO of Berkshire Hathaway, in the firm's 1994 annual report.*

Downsizing

It really astonishes me how many chief executives don't have the gumption to fire corporate deadwood. In large companies employing large numbers, you find expensive, titled executives tucked away in nooks and crannies and cupboards. They are a drain in more ways than just their own salary. Failing to fire management deadwood burdens the rest of the working workers as well as the stockholders.

> **FRANK BORMAN,** *CEO of Eastern Airlines, in 1978.*

We have not laid off or furloughed a single employee for lack of work for more than twenty-five years. Most of our plants are located in small towns and rural areas. We cannot just lay people off, because they have no place to go.

> **F. KENNETH IVERSON,** *CEO of U.S. steel maker Nucor, one of the few consistently profitable steelmakers in the U.S. in recent decades, in a 1996 speech.*

It seems to me that when external realities create changes in the market, which your employees are not responsible for, then as a manager your obligation is to find a way to retrain and redeploy those employees, rather than saying, "Oops, the market's changed, too bad, gang, that's not our fault either, you're fired." Because when you do that, you're still sitting there in the executive offices. That doesn't seem right.

> IRVINE O. HOCKADAY JR., *CEO of Hallmark Cards of Kansas City, in* Fortune *in 1987, on the firm's no-layoffs policy. The firm had not imposed a layoff since it was founded by Joyce Hall in 1910.*

If you fire people, you fire customers.

> FERDINAND PIECH, *CEO of German auto maker Volkswagen, in the 1990s.*

These big billionaires are busy letting go managers in their fifties, the day before their pension plans kick in. We're getting to be like Mexico and Brazil, with the rich living behind fences, like they do in Hollywood. All the money is in the hands of these few rich people and none of them give any money away. It's dangerous for them and for the country. We may have another French Revolution and there'll be another Madame Defarge knitting and watching them come in little oxcarts down to the town square and BOOM! Off with their heads!

> TED TURNER, *interviewed by Maureen Dowd of the* New York Times *in 1996.*

REALITY CHECK

We tend to meet any new situation by reorganization and attribute to this the illusion that progress is being made.

PETRONIUS ARBITER, *AD 66*

It is a criminal sin for a company to make an announcement one morning that they are letting 22 percent—or some such number—of their workforce go. You have got to ask yourself: Where the hell was management? How did they get 22 percent too many people?

> **SAMUEL L. EICHENFELD,** *CEO of U.S. financial services firm Finova Group, in Charles B. Wendel's,* The New Financiers: Profiles of the Leaders Who Are Reshaping the Financial Services Industry *(1996).*

Depopulate. Get rid of people. They gum up the works.

> **JEFFREY SKILLING,** *president of U.S. energy-trading firm Enron, in the* Financial Times *in 1997. Skilling abruptly quit Enron in August 2001, only a few months after becoming CEO. In December of that year, Enron filed for Chapter 11 protection from its creditors—the biggest bankruptcy in U.S. history.*

If you have to show a report card at the end of the day about how much blood you've spilled on the street, then why would anyone want to work for you? Why would anyone trust you in the future if you're just a synergy victim waiting to happen?

> **ROB HAIN**, *CEO of AIM Funds Management, Canada's second-largest mutual fund manager, in the* Financial Post *in 2001.*

Ego

Vanity began to whisper to me that I was of some importance, and my beloved tutor often warned me against its siren power.

> **REBECCA WEBB LUKENS**, *first female CEO of an industrial company in the United States, who in the early 19th century inherited a faltering boilerplate maker, Brandywine Iron Works of Coatesville, Pennsylvania, and rescued the firm, which survives as Lukens, the United States' oldest continuously operating steel mill.*

It is very vulgar to talk about one's business. Only people like stockbrokers do that, and then merely at dinner parties.

> **JOHN WANAMAKER**, *19th-century Philadelphia department store pioneer.*

That's because I wasn't there.

> **HENRY J. KAISER**, *U.S. West Coast industrialist, famed for turning out warships at a record pace during World War II, to a balky subordinate who argued that a deadline could not be met because, after all, "Rome wasn't built in a day."*

I'm the Medici to my own Leonardo.

> **JOHN CALVIN PORTMAN**, *who broke with architects' no-developing creed by developing his own large-scale projects, notably U.S. hotels in the 1970s with trademark soaring cylindrical atria.*

Remember, we're in a hall of mirrors. To succeed, you must avoid the trap of being overly dazzled by your own image.

> **JOHN R. BECKETT**, *chairman of U.S. financial services firm Transamerica, in a 1981 commencement address at the University of Santa Clara.*

A full moon blanks out all the stars around it.

> **TED TURNER**, *U.S. media mogul, on his impact on the TV industry.*

I don't want to be part of a book. I'm just a grungy, lousy manager.

> **JACK WELCH**, *CEO of General Electric, in the early 1980s, soon after taking the helm, to Ralph Nader, who wanted to interview him for a book.*

REALITY CHECK

Hoy-day, what a sweep of vanity comes this way!

> **WILLIAM SHAKESPEARE**

You can't sell successfully to the black consumer without me.

> **JOHN H. JOHNSON,** *publisher of* Ebony, *in Robert Sobel and David B. Sicilia's,* The Entrepreneurs: An American Adventure *(1986).*

What I have done is build the most beautiful buildings in the best locations. What good is it if no one knows about it?

> **DONALD TRUMP,** *New York developer, in the 1990s, on his penchant for self-promotion.*

I don't design sleeves and jackets. I design a world.

> **RALPH LAUREN,** *U.S. fashion designer, in* Forbes *in 1991.*

I can look at a CEO's week's agenda and see if he's got an ego problem. If a guy stays out of Washington, doesn't go to a lot of dinner parties, and always goes to operating reviews, his ego's okay.

> **LARRY BOSSIDY,** *CEO of U.S. conglomerate AlliedSignal, in the 1990s.*

I'm a superstar in my field, much like Michael Jordan in basketball and Bruce Springsteen in rock 'n' roll.

> **ALBERT J. (CHAINSAW AL) DUNLAP,** *CEO of U.S. tissue maker Scott Paper, in his 1996 memoir,* Mean Business. *A few years later, Dunlap was fired as CEO of U.S. appliance maker Sunbeam, after his turnaround effort ended in failure amid charges of improper accounting methods.*

According to my mom, I'm such a big shot that she's threatening to have her uterus bronzed.

> **STEVEN SPIELBERG**, *filmmaker and co-owner of film studio Dreamworks, whose reputation as Hollywood's most bankable director began with the box office hit* Jaws *in 1975.*

I am proud to be part of an industry that has revolutionized the world in only twenty-five years. The computer software industry has produced more new products and services at affordable prices, created more economic opportunity, and empowered more people than any other industry at any other time in history.

> **BILL GATES**, *CEO of Microsoft, 1998 testimony to a U.S. Senate committee on antitrust allegations against his firm. Gates shared with many peers a belief that computer software's contributions to civilization outranked those of the rail, auto, and telephone eras.*

There is no one in Europe or in the world who can match me for my talents or personal background. None of the political players have my past.

> **SILVIO BERLUSCONI**, *Italian media mogul, who began his career as a singer on cruise ships, in his successful 2001 campaign to become Italy's prime minister.*

Viacom is me.

> **SUMNER REDSTONE**, *founder of U.S. media conglomerate Viacom, owner of Paramount Pictures and the CBS television network, first line of his 2001 memoir,* A Passion to Win.

Empowerment

Those men to whom we delegate authority and responsibility, if they are good men, are going to have ideas of their own and are going to want to do their jobs in their own way. Management that is destructively critical when mistakes are made kills initiative, and it's essential that we have many people with initiative if we are to continue to grow.

> WILLIAM L. MCKNIGHT, *builder of the modern 3M (formally Minnesota Mining and Manufacturing), in a memo from the 1950s.*

We have found out that we cannot trust some people who are nonconformists. We will make conformists out of them in a hurry. The organization cannot trust the individual; the individual must trust the organization [or] he shouldn't go into this kind of business.

> RAY KROC, *founder of McDonald's, in 1958, describing his oversight of new franchisees.*

This is a basic and simple business. People create problems by not trusting their own judgment. By creating a committee. By constantly needing validation. You guys are empowered. You can find 99 percent of the answers in the aisles, where the customers are.

> BERNARD MARCUS, *co-founder of U.S. retailer Home Depot, with a message to employees in* Fortune *in 1996.*

If you empower dummies, you get bad decisions faster.

> RICK TEERLINK, *CEO of Harley-Davidson, in 1994, disparaging faddish management theories.*

Nordstom Rules:
Rule #1: Use your own good judgment in all situations.
There will be no additional rules.

> BRUCE, JIM, AND JOHN NORDSTROM, *brothers and co-presidents of U.S. department store retailer Nordstrom, employee handbook, in its entirety, printed on a five by eight-inch card, in the 1990s.*

I admire your system in the United States, but you have to recognize that Japan is very different. We at Toyota would have a lot of problems with entry-level people who are too unstructured in their thinking.

> HIROSHI OKUDA, *chairman of Toyota, asked at a mid-1990s talk with management students at Yale University if the tradition at Japanese universities to discourage independent thinking had a negative impact. Cited in Jeffrey E. Garten's,* The Mind of the C.E.O. *(2001).*

I began with a philosophy that we could create an environment where leaders felt empowered. Now, I'm not trusting in people so much.

> CHRISTOPHER B. GALVIN, *CEO of Motorola, an electronics firm based in Schaumberg, Illinois, in* Business Week *in 2001, on taking back authority from top managers who had failed in their responsibilities.*

Environment

Some products are really outrageous chemicals such as acetone, acetaldehyde, methyl butyrate, ethyl caproate, hexyl acetate, methanol, acrolein and even that stuff called crotonaldehyde. How dare anybody come up with a product with all those chemicals? Well, that would be a problem because the product I've described is a fresh strawberry, naturally grown, with no man-made ingredients.

> **R.F. HERBERT**, *CEO of U.S. chemical giant DuPont, in a 1989 speech.*

No matter how brilliant the technological revolutions, no matter how useful the economic and political initiatives, there can only be hope if man can cast away his anthropocentric delusions and seek to find his place in nature, a place from which he can live in harmony with his universe.

> **SIR JAMES GOLDSMITH**, *corporate raider turned environmentalist, in 1989. After amassing a fortune from paper companies that cut wide swaths through the forests, Goldsmith was persuaded by his brother, Teddy, to become a crusading environmentalist in the 1990s.*

The white European-descent people…we're the ones that have destroyed the world.

> **TED TURNER**, *U.S. media mogul, in* Forbes *in 1991.*

We are able to find and measure smaller and smaller quantities of toxic materials. For example, dioxin is produced in pulp and paper in quantities so extremely minute that we have only recently been able to detect them. One part per quadrillion—the quantities that we are talking of—is like one second in thirty-two million years. We are committed to reducing dioxin levels to non-detectable levels. But what is non-detectable? It just means that we can't detect it today. Tomorrow, as we advance our technology, we may be able to measure it again.

> MARSHALL HAHN, *CEO of U.S. forest products company Georgia-Pacific and a PhD in physics, in* Fortune *in 1990.*

Who could have imagined ten years ago what people would sacrifice for a cleaner environment? Almost half of our $25 billion annual sales are directly or indirectly related to environmental issues. The greenhouse effect, global warming, and the ozone layer are high on the political agenda in western Europe. In eastern Europe, the environmental destruction is horrifying. Its countries need to totally rebuild their energy systems. That means even more opportunity.

> PERCY BARNEVIK, *president of ABB, a Swedish-Swiss joint venture that provides engineering services and electrical equipment worldwide, in* Fortune *in 1990.*

I've staked much of my personal reputation on the environment. Sometimes I wake up wondering whether I'm taking the company on a diversionary course that won't pay off. But on other nights I wake up thinking we're not doing enough.

> WILLIAM CLAY (BILL) FORD JR., *chairman of Ford Motor, in Jeffrey E. Garten's,* The Mind of the C.E.O. *(2001). In the late 1990s, Ford stunned Motown auto executives by musing that gas-guzzling sport utility vehicles, upon which Ford Motor was conspicuously dependent for profits, might be harmful to the environment.*

Ethics

When you cannot make pure goods of full weight, go to something else that is honest, even if it is breaking stone.

> JAMES GAMBLE, *co-founder with William Procter in 1837 of Cincinnati-based Procter & Gamble, in the mid-19th century. The early P&G gained an edge over rival soap-makers in Cincinnati by giving honest weight and consistent quality.*

People believe in the man. I have known a man to come into my office, and I have given him a check for a million dollars when I knew he had not a cent in the world. The first thing is character. Before money or property or anything else. Money cannot buy it, because a man I do not trust would not get money out of me on all the bonds in Christendom.

> J. P. MORGAN, *U.S. financier, testifying at a congressional inquiry into his bailout of financial houses during the panic of 1907.*

Tell them the truth, first because it is the right thing to do and second they'll find out anyway.

> **PAUL GALVIN**, *founder of Motorola, an electronics firm based in Schaumberg, Illinois, in the 1930s, when it was common practice to exaggerate a company's financial health and the quality of its products to skeptical distributors.*

What was the point of a contract? I couldn't have made a down payment anyway.

> **C. R. (CYRUS ROWLETT) SMITH**, *CEO of a capital-starved American Airlines, who concluded his purchase of twenty-five DC-3 airplanes from Donald Douglas with a mere handshake.*

In my book, an S.O.B. is someone who uses whatever tactics it takes to get the job done—to rise to the top.

> **AL NEUHARTH**, *former CEO of U.S. newspaper chain Gannett, in his 1989 memoir,* Confessions of an S.O.B. *When his first big promotion came at the* Miami Herald, *Neuharth got the managing editor to delay it until he could work in every department so that his co-workers would unwittingly confide in their future boss.*

Never play by the rules. Never pay in cash and never tell the truth.

> **F. ROSS JOHNSON**, *CEO of RJR Nabisco, in the 1980s.*

Play by the rules, but be ferocious.

> **PHIL KNIGHT**, *founder of U.S. sportswear firm Nike, in the 1980s.*

Mozer's paying $30,000 and is sentenced to prison for four months. Salomon's shareholders—including me—paid $290 million, and I got sentenced to ten months as CEO.

> **WARREN BUFFETT**, *CEO of Berkshire Hathaway, in 1994, on how he was forced to become interim CEO of Berkshire-controlled Salomon, an investment dealer, after a scandal over U.S. Treasury bond auctions triggered by Salomon trader Paul Mozer.*

We want to be proud of Enron and to know that it enjoys a reputation for fairness and honesty and that it is respected. Gaining such respect is one aim of our advertising and public relations activities, but no matter how effective they may be, Enron's reputation finally depends on its people, on you and me. Let's keep that reputation high.

> **KENNETH L. LAY**, *CEO of Enron, in the preface to the company's late-1990s code of ethics. After Enron's bankruptcy in 2001 amid allegations of accounting irregularities, the sixty-four-page ethics code was offered as a collector's item on the eBay auction site for $160.*

I always took the attitude that I was being misled. If I went into a meeting with a company and it turned out they were telling the truth, I was pleasantly surprised.

> **SALLIE KRAWCHECK**, *CEO of Sanford C. Bernstein, a leading U.S. stock-research advisor to institutional investors, in* Fortune *in 2002. Krawcheck recalled a Merrill Lynch tour in Japan in which securities analysts were shown a busy Merrill retail branch. Acting on a hunch, she visited other Merrill offices and found that business was dead. Merrill later scaled back its money-losing Japanese operation.*

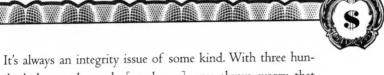

It's always an integrity issue of some kind. With three hundred thousand people [employees], you always worry that somebody doesn't get it. We can survive bad markets. What you can't live through is anybody who takes from the company or does something wrong in the community.

JEFFREY R. IMMELT, *CEO of General Electric, asked by* Business Week *in 2002 what keeps him up at night.*

I've been in business for forty years—twenty-five or thirty years in senior management. And I find myself feeling embarrassed and ashamed by what I see in corporate America. The same way the market sentiment shifted toward an unbridled exuberance, the values of a lot of people managing companies in their market environment drifted toward 'Me, me, me.' "

ANDREW GROVE, *Chairman of U.S. semiconductor-maker Intel Corp., in the* New York Times *in 2002, on the reports of excessive pay collected by CEOs of failing enterprises. Between 1985 and 2001, average pay for CEOs in the U.S. increased by 866 percent, while pay for the average worker rose by just 63 percent.*

It's the same thing as when a couple of policemen are found corrupt. The whole police department suffers.

JEAN-PIERRE GARNIER, *CEO of Anglo-American drug company GlaxoSmithKline, in the* New York Times *in 2002, on the proliferation of CEOs facing allegations of unethical conduct, and a resulting loss of confidence in corporate leadership.*

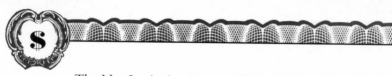

The No. 1 criterion in every CEO search we do today is integrity. That used to be assumed. No one had to mention it. Not anymore.

> GERALD R. ROCHE, *Senior Chairman of leading U.S. executive recruitment firm Heidrick & Struggles, in the* New York Times *in 2002, about the aftermath of high-profile accounting scandals and other improprieties at a multitude of companies including Enron, Xerox, Tyco International, QWest, Global Crossing, ImClone Systems, and Adelphia Communications.*

Failure

The fastest way to succeed is to double your failure rate.

> THOMAS J. WATSON SR., *founder of the modern IBM, who joined the company in 1914.*

If you have made mistakes, even serious ones, there is always another chance for you. What we call failure is not the falling down, but the staying down.

> MARY PICKFORD, *Canadian-born U.S. actor and co-founder in 1919 of United Artists Films with Charlie Chaplin, D.W. Griffiths, and Douglas Fairbanks.*

Success represents the 1 percent of your work that results from the 99 percent that is called failure.

> SOICHIRO HONDA, *founder in 1946 of Japanese automaker Honda.*

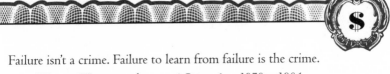

Failure isn't a crime. Failure to learn from failure is the crime.

WALTER WRISTON, *chairman of Citicorp from 1970 to 1984.*

Isn't it wonderful that we live in a country where a major summer story [last year] was not woe and misery, but something so deliciously benign as a soft drink. A soft drink that the American public suddenly fell in love with all over again. "Hey, that's ours," they said. "Give it back."

ROBERTO C. GOIZUETA, *CEO of Coca-Cola. The firm's decision to reformulate its flagship product in 1985 was one of the great marketing disasters of the century.*

The majority of the things we do fail. The fact that anything comes out the door is a tribute to the tremendous tenacity of hundreds of people.

DR. P. ROY VAGELOS, *CEO of U.S. pharmaceutical company Merck & Co., in* Business Week *in 1987.*

Failing is good as long as it doesn't become a habit.

MICHAEL D. EISNER, *CEO of Walt Disney Co., in a 1996 speech.*

If at first you don't succeed…welcome to the club.

ISRAEL HAROLD (IZZY) ASPER, *media magnate, upon being inducted into the Canadian Business Hall of Fame in the mid-1990s.*

REALITY CHECK

Not failure, but low aim is crime.

JAMES RUSSELL LOWELL

If the chairman can buy Kidder Peabody and mess it up, you can do just about anything. If the chairman can do that and still survive, you ought to be able to take swings everywhere. You can hardly do worse.

> **JACK WELCH**, *Chairman and CEO of General Electric, for whom the purchase of securities firm Kidder Peabody resulted in a $1.2 billion write-off, in 2001.*

It's okay to have a company fail, and to start again. At least it is in Silicon Valley. Sometimes you don't even have to change the place where you park your car.

> **JOHN DOERR**, *partner at California venture capital firm Kleiner Perkins Caufield and Byers, in 2001.*

This is the only business where you can crash and burn cataclysmically in the winter—and the next summer return to the same stage with a giant home run. I like to say that I'm in a business where failure is an inevitable cul-de-sac on the road to success.

> **PETER GRUBER**, *head of Mandalay, a Hollywood production company, and former chairman of Sony Pictures, interviewed in* Slate *in 2002.*

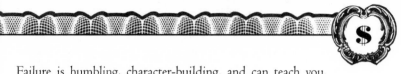

Failure is humbling, character-building, and can teach you, but it is definitely not good.

> **JULIE WAINWRIGHT**, *CEO of Pets.com, an early dot-com failure, in the* Wall Street Journal *in 2002.*

Family Business

I have a theory of relatives too—don't hire 'em.

> **JACK L. WARNER**, *Canadian-born co-founder in 1923 of Warner Bros., to Albert Einstein during the scientist's tour of the Warner studio.*

God damn you, old man! Can't you ever leave me alone?

> **THOMAS J. WATSON JR.**, *to his father. The father and son, successive heads of IBM, broke off a public shouting match, only for Watson Sr. to chase his son in a limousine to the airport, where they continued the argument.*

Tell me, Edgar, are we buying all this stock in MGM just so you can get laid?

> **SAMUEL BRONFMAN**, *CEO of liquor giant Seagram, in the late 1960s, who opposed son Edgar's interest in buying a Hollywood studio. Edgar's reply: "Oh, no, Pop, it doesn't cost $40 million to get laid."*

The Saudi royal family likes dealing one dynasty to another.

> **STEVEN DAVISON BECHTEL JR.**, *CEO of giant U.S. engineering firm Bechtel, on why his firm clung to its private, family-owned status, in the 1980s.*

There were board meetings when my wife was doing needle-point, one sister was addressing Christmas cards, and another sister didn't bother to attend.

> **BARRY BINGHAM JR.**, *co-inheritor of his family's Louisville, Kentucky-based newspaper business, in 1986 on the acrimony among family members that led to the company's sale to an outside party.*

I want to thank our host for omitting from the reasons for my rapid rise the most important of all, the fact that my dad owns the joint.

> **ROBERT W. GALVIN**, *CEO of Motorola, a firm founded by his father, Paul Galvin, in Schaumberg, Illinois, with a characteristic opening line to one of his public speeches.*

I'd rather be a pianist, a national treasure, but it didn't work out that way.

> **MICKEY ARISON**, *who succeeded his father, Carnival Cruise Line founder Ted Arison, as head of the family firm, in the 1980s.*

My mother gave me everything but an easy act to follow.

> **DONALD GRAHAM**, *on succeeding his mother, Katharine Graham, as publisher of the* Washington Post, *in* Media People *in 1986.*

The family is like a train—I am the engine and the others are the wagons.

> **ALDO GUCCI**, *Italian fashion mogul, on the fractious Gucci clan.*

I was brought up with an ethic that when you got up each morning it was to achieve something. Otherwise, you're a failure. That's a pretty good background, if it doesn't crack you.

> **GALEN WESTON**, *controlling shareholder of Loblaw, Canada's largest grocery chain, in 1988. Weston was a protégé of his father, Garfield, who built an empire of bakery and grocery firms in North America, Europe, South Africa, and Australia.*

Is there any day of the year when you're really free? Not with this kind of responsibility. Our name won't remain internationally known if we are nincompoops.

> **PETER WALLENBERG**, *patriarch of Sweden's dominant industrial family, in* Time *in 1996.*

I wasn't driven to acting by an inner compulsion. I was running away from the sporting goods business.

> **PAUL NEWMAN**, *actor, philanthropist, and entrepreneur, who inherited a sporting-goods store in Cleveland and sold it as soon as he could. Only much later did he return to business with a nonprofit food products company, Newman's Own, whose earnings were donated to various charities.*

Nepotism is the most efficient way of running a business. But it has to be enlightened nepotism.

> **NICKY OPPENHEIMER**, *third-generation CEO of De Beers Consolidated Mines, who was training his son Jonathan to succeed him, in London's* Financial Times *in 2001.*

I don't want to blame my father for anything, but it was the first time I woke up in the morning and wanted to get out of bed.

> **GARRY WESTON**, *CEO of London-based Associated British Foods, a food conglomerate that owns the Ryvita, Wagon Wheel cookies, Silver Spoon Sugar brands, and the upscale store Fortnum and Mason, cited in his 2002 obituary in Britain's* Guardian *on his self-exile to Australia in the 1950s to run the family's operations there, free of his father's exacting scrutiny.*

Feedback

Once a junior executive made a serious error. After I read to him my official reprimand letter, I told him he was lucky to have someone to tell him off. "If I made such a mistake," I said, "there is no one who would say anything right to me, but you can bet there would be a lot of criticism behind my back. And I would go on making the same error. Once you are promoted to top positions, no one is going to protest, no matter what you do."

> **KONOSUKE MATSUSHITA**, *founder of Matsushita Electric Industrial, maker of Panasonic, Technics, and Quasar products, in the 1970s.*

Gentlemen, I've been thinking. Bull times zero is bull. Bull divided by zero is infinity bull. And I'm sick and tired of the bull you've been feeding me.

> **HAROLD S. GENEEN**, *CEO of U.S. conglomerate ITT, in the* New York Times *in 1971, admonishing his lieutenants.*

It's really the heart of the issue: Can we take the punitive aspects out of having people tell us the truth?

> **JACK WELCH**, *CEO of General Electric, in the early 1980s, soon after taking the helm.*

Anybody incapable of punching me in the face is probably incapable of being a group executive for Grand Met.

> **ALLEN SHEPPARD**, *CEO of British drinks and hospitality conglomerate Grand Metropolitan, in the 1980s.*

I wanted a picture…of a worker talking to his foreman. We had fourteen thousand photos in the file, but not one of a supervisor *listening* to a worker.

> **RENE MCPHERSON**, *CEO of Ohio-based auto-parts maker Dana, in Thomas J. Peters and Robert H. Waterman Jr.'s,* In Search of Excellence: Lessons from America's Best-Run Companies *(1982).*

I looked for those sharp, scratchy, harsh, almost unpleasant guys who see and tell you about things as they really are.

> **THOMAS J. WATSON JR.**, *CEO of IBM, in* Fortune *in 1987.*

REALITY CHECK

Woe unto you, when all men shall speak well of you.

> **LUKE** 6:26

One of the worst things we do in corporate America is not tell people what we think of them.... I think it's healthy to let all the [employee] frustration get aired. It's good if people go home at night and say, "I told that son of a bitch what I thought of him today."

> **LARRY BOSSIDY**, *CEO of AlliedSignal, in* Harvard Business Review *in 1995.*

You never really hear the truth from your subordinates until after ten in the evening.

> **JURGEN SCHREMPP**, *CEO of Daimler-Benz, later DaimlerChrysler, in the* Economist *in 1996.*

One of the dangers [of being CEO] is to become corrupted in the way you judge yourself and to stop listening to critics or being honest about your shortcomings.

> **DR. DANIEL VASELLA**, *CEO of Swiss pharmaceuticals group Novartis, in the* Financial Times *in 2001.*

Firing

Sometimes you just don't like somebody.

> **HENRY FORD II**, *chairman of Ford Motor, when asked by the CEO heir apparent why he fired Ford president Lee Iacocca, in 1978.*

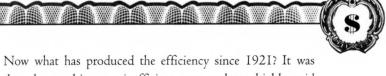

Now what has produced the efficiency since 1921? It was done by combing out inefficient men, and too highly paid men, elderly men, and men past their work steadily for the last three years, and I am confident that this has produced a state of "fear" in the minds of the remainder that if they were not efficient their turn would come next.

> **WILLIAM LEVER, LORD LEVERHULME,** *CEO of British consumer products firm Lever Bros. (later Unilever), in 1924, on his campaign to prune the managerial ranks with overt zeal as a warning to slackers.*

I just wanted to see what a room full of sons of bitches looks like.

> **NEIL MCKINNON,** *CEO of Canadian Imperial Bank of Commerce, confronting members of the bank's board of directors who had ousted him a few hours earlier, in 1973.*

Boy, thirty-eight years old, president of C&S. I thought I had the world by the tail. I thought I had all the answers, and I got knocked off that platform. You learn very quickly that you don't have all the answers.

> **RICHARD L. KATTEL,** *ousted as CEO of Atlanta-based Citizens & Southern National Bank in 1978.*

Show me a man who enjoys firing people and I'll show you a charlatan or a sadist.

> **ANTHONY O'REILLY,** *CEO of H.J. Heinz, in* Business Week *in 1987.*

You'd better start firing people so they'll understand you're serious.

> LINDA WACHNER, *CEO of intimate-apparel maker Warnaco, to one of her top managers soon after gaining control of the firm in a leveraged buyout. Cited in* Fortune *in 1993. Wachner herself was fired by the Warnaco board in 2001, a few months after the company filed for bankruptcy.*

Reality Check

In this country, we find it pays to shoot an admiral from time to time to encourage the others.

> VOLTAIRE, *Candide*

Take your chairman into a corner and shoot him quickly— we don't want the fuss of a public trial.

> MAURICE SAATCHI, *co-founder of British ad agency Saatchi & Saatchi, in a 1995 letter to employees, describing how he had just been fired from his own company.*

Generally speaking, you like to dance with the girl that brung you, and if you can't, sometimes you have to shoot her.

> DAVID BONDERMAN, *owner of Continental Airlines, on why he sacked the chief of a subsidiary, in* Business Week *in 1996.*

A company that bets its future on its people must remove that lower 10 percent, and keep removing it every year—always raising the bar of performance and increasing the quality of its leadership.

> JACK WELCH, *CEO of General Electric, in 2001.*

Fitness and Health

Sleep is a colossal waste of time.

> THOMAS EDISON, *inventor and founder of a forerunner company to General Electric in the late 19th century.*

Capitalists are supposed to be possessive individualists, right? Well, the only thing an entrepreneur doesn't have is a possessive, individualist attitude toward is his own body. The most extreme capitalists in fact give up themselves. They share communally their body, their health, their peace of mind.

> MOSES ZNAIMER, *co-founder of Toronto's Citytv, in Alexander Ross, The Risk Takers (1975).*

For exercise, I wind my watch.

> ROBERT MAXWELL, *Czech-born British publishing tycoon, in* Time *in 1988. Maxwell died a few years later, an apparent suicide, just before his publishing empire collapsed.*

I get my exercise acting as a pallbearer to my friends who exercise.

CHAUNCEY DEPEW, *New York Central Railroad chairman in the early 1900s who lived to be 94, in* Forbes *in 1986.*

Tired people make bad decisions.... When I woke up at four in the morning, I [wrote] down what was worrying me. Then I could feel better and go back to sleep.

RICHARD (DICK) JENRETTE, *manager of successful turnarounds at U.S. brokerage firm Donaldson Lufkin Jenrette and insurer Equitable, in* Fortune *in 1996.*

People always go on a diet 'Monday.' On Friday: "I'm going on a diet Monday because I'm going to two restaurants this weekend." On Sunday they renegotiate.

RUTH FERTEL, *founder of the Ruth's Chris Steak House chain, explaining in a New Orleans magazine interview in 1997 that the beef business is invulnerable to health trends. In 2001, Fertel's chain had eighty-two outlets and sales of $328 million.*

For many years I dealt with stress by dancing. I hoofed, I strutted and pranced and boogied and stomped and shimmied and sometimes I slipped in a hula or a tango. I shook until I could get out of my head and into the tub. Then I would sit in the water, a zombie. The best song I ever found for shaking my psyche into shape was "I Will Survive." It's still better than any pill.

MARY WELLS LAWRENCE, *co-founder in 1966 of New York advertising agency Wells Rich Greene, in 2002.*

Hiring

Oh Lord, give me a bastard with talent.

> **CHARLES REVSON**, *co-founder of U.S. cosmetics giant Revlon, on his search for recruits with a killer instinct, in Andrew Tobias's* Fire and Ice: The Story of Charles Revson—The Man Who Built the Revlon Empire *(1975).*

Do you want to spend the rest of your life selling sugared water or do you want a chance to change the world?

> **STEVE JOBS**, *co-founder of Apple, recruiting John Sculley, forty-two, from PepsiCo to be Apple's president, in 1983.*

If you hire the best people and leave them alone, you don't need to hire very many.

> **THOMAS S. (SAWYER) MURPHY**, *CEO of U.S. broadcaster Capital Cities/ABC, in the late 1980s. In the mid-1990s, Murphy sold the company to Walt Disney Co.*

I believe in the adage: Hire people smarter than you and get out of their way.

> **HOWARD SCHULTZ**, *founder of the Starbucks coffee chain, in* Business Week *in 1994.*

A's hire A's, B's hire C's.

> **DONALD RUMSFELD**, *former CEO of drugmaker G.D. Searle & Co. and twice U.S. Secretary of Defense, in 2001.*

Some [prospective employees] choose ten ties that are really the worst. If he does that, then we move on to the scarves. If he is bad with the scarves, well, then he is really in a difficult position.

> **BERNARD ARNAULT**, *CEO of Paris-based luxury goods marketer LVMH Moët Hennessy Louis Vuitton, on testing job candidates who are asked to select ten good ties from one hundred, in the* New York Times *in 1997.*

We tried to hire people because they believed in what the company was doing. We were looking for what we call missionaries, as opposed to mercenaries. In Silicon Valley, a lot of companies were founded by mercenaries, and they were not built to last. They were built to flip.

> **MARGARET C. (MEG) WHITMAN**, *CEO of U.S. online auction firm eBay, in* Business Week *in 2001.*

If you have to choose between someone with a staggering I.Q. and an elite education who's gliding along, and someone with a lower I.Q., but who is absolutely determined to succeed, you'll always do better with the second person.

> **LARRY BOSSIDY**, *CEO of Honeywell, with Ram Charan in their 2002 book,* Execution: The Discipline of Getting Things Done.

Ideas

It behooves no-one to dismiss any novel idea with the statement that it "can't be done." Our job is to keep everlastingly at research and experiment, to adapt our laboratories to production as soon as practicable, to let no new improvement in flying and flying equipment pass us by.

> WILLIAM E. (BILL) BOEING, *CEO of U.S. aircraft maker Boeing. The motto appears on a bronze plaque at the firm's former headquarters in Seattle, where Bill Boeing founded the company in 1915.*

If you want to kill any idea around the world today, get a committee working on it.

> CHARLES FRANKLIN KETTERING, *20th-century U.S. inventor, industrialist and philanthropist, and a partner with Alfred P. Sloan Jr. in building General Motors.*

The job of all good chief executives is to destroy good ideas.

> PETER JOB, *CEO of Reuters, the London-based news and information purveyor, in the 1990s.*

Big ideas are so hard to recognize, so fragile, so easy to kill. Don't forget that, all of you who don't have them.

> JOHN ELLIOTT JR., *parting words on retiring as chairman of ad agency Ogilvy & Mather International, in the 1990s.*

I love it when front-line employees come up with ideas, because I know they are the things that generally work.

> **RAKESH GANGWAL**, *CEO of US Airways Group, interviewed in* The New York Times *in 2000.*

We tell people that if you need a suggestion box then you're not doing what you should be doing. You shouldn't have to interpose a box between you and the people with ideas. You ought to be with your people enough that they are comfortable to just pop on in and give you their ideas.

> **HERB KELLEHER**, *co-founder and CEO of Dallas-based Southwest Airlines, the only consistently profitable major airline in the world in the 1990s, interviewed in* Fortune *in 2001.*

Imposter Syndrome

Fake it till you make it.

> **MARY KAY ASH**, *founder in 1963 of Dallas-based cosmetics marketer Mary Kay Cosmetics.*

Everyone who's running something goes home at night and wrestles with the same fear: *Am I going to be the one who blows this place up?*

> **JACK WELCH**, *CEO of General Electric, in 2001.*

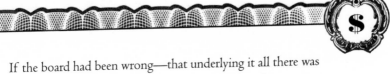

If the board had been wrong—that underlying it all there was a technical problem in IBM—then it would have been a very short tenure for me.

> **LOUIS V. GERSTNER JR.,** *CEO of IBM from 1993 to 2002, in the* New York Times *in 2002. Called in to spearhead a turnaround of the iconic firm, Gerstner lacked a technical background, having previously worked at consulting firm McKinsey and as CEO of American Express and RJR Nabisco.*

The only time I think about being a businesswoman is now, while I'm talking to you. There's this part of me that's afraid of what will happen if I believe it.

> **OPRAH WINFREY,** *90 percent owner of Chicago-based production company Harpo, interviewed about her $988 million entertainment empire in* Fortune *in 2002.*

Inheritance

Inherited wealth is death to ambition, as cocaine is to morality.

> **WILLIAM VANDERBILT,** *grandson and heir to the immense railroad fortune of 19th-century industrialist Cornelius Vanderbilt.*

My rise to the top was through sheer ability and inheritance.

> **MALCOLM FORBES,** *CEO of U.S. magazine publisher Forbes Inc., who inherited the business from his father, B. C. Forbes, in the 1980s.*

You can be obnoxious if you made it yourself. But I have to remember where the wealth came from.

> **HOWARD KASKEL**, *New York developer who inherited his father's Doral Hotel chain in 1968 and whose own net worth was estimated at $275 million in 1986.*

REALITY CHECK

Saving is a very fine thing, especially when your parents have done it for you.

> **WINSTON CHURCHILL**

If your kids grow up living in fairyland thinking that they're princes and princesses, you're going to curse their lives.

> **H. ROSS PEROT**, *founder of Electronic Data Systems, in* Fortune *in 1986, on fears of raising children who are unable to survive without their inheritance.*

All these people who think that food stamps are debilitating and lead to a cycle of poverty, they're the same ones who go out and want to leave a ton of money to their kids.

> **WARREN BUFFETT**, *CEO of Berkshire Hathaway, in the* San Diego Union-Tribune *in 1994.*

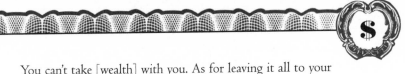

You can't take [wealth] with you. As for leaving it all to your kids, is it necessary, is it wise, do you want to drip acid on their heads constantly?

> ROBERT KUOK, *Chinese billionaire industrialist, in* Forbes *in 1997.*

Innovation

Anything that won't sell, I don't want to invent. Its sale is proof of utility, and utility is success.

> THOMAS EDISON, *U.S. inventor and industrialist, founder of Edison General Electric in the late 19th century, a forerunner to General Electric, and holder of 1,093 patents.*

For twenty years we protected ourselves with a variety of rubber coats, hats, lap robes, and other makeshift things. For some reason or other, it took us a long time to realize that the way to keep dry in a motorcar was to keep the weather out of the car.

> ALFRED P. (PRITCHARD) SLOAN JR., *founder of the modern General Motors, head of GM for two decades beginning in the 1920s, and a pioneer in enclosed passenger cabins, on the slow pace of innovation in the auto industry.*

Before you build a better mousetrap, it helps to know if there are any mice out there.

> MORTIMER ZUCKERMAN, *real estate and media investor, in the 1980s.*

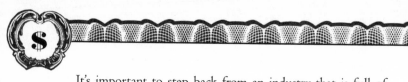

It's important to step back from an industry that is full of people announcing new widgets every day—faster widgets, smaller widgets, more widgets. What I'm learning from customers is that there is an excess of technology out there. The real pressure is, how do I use this stuff to achieve something important for my business?

LOUIS V. GERSTNER JR., *CEO of IBM, in* Fortune *in 1993.*

Fifty percent of the developments we try don't work out. We don't publicize our failures. When something doesn't work out, don't leave the corpse lying around. We like the saying, "If it's worth doing, it's worth doing poorly." Don't study the idea to death with experts and committees. Get on with it, and see if it works.

F. KENNETH IVERSON, *CEO of U.S. steel maker Nucor, in a 1996 speech.*

Elwood Haynes, of Kokomo, Indiana, is often credited with the invention of the automobile. But no one drove here today in a Haynes. The lesson of history is that innovation is a necessary condition for business success—but not a sufficient condition for business success.

RANDALL L. TOBIAS, *CEO of Indianapolis-based drug giant Eli Lilly, in a 1997 speech.*

Come quickly; I am tasting stars!

> **DOM PÉRIGNON**, *17th-century Benedictine monk and a pioneer in the cultivation of grapes. According to legend, these were his words upon inventing the sparkling wine later known as champagne.*

Internet

This thing is like a tidal wave. If you fail in the game, you're going to be dead.

> **HUGH MCCOLL**, *CEO of Nationsbank, in the* Wall Street Journal *in 1996, on the Internet.*

The Internet is only surpassed by mental telepathy.

> **BILL GATES**, *co-founder of Microsoft, in the late 1990s.*

I was afraid of the Internet because I couldn't type.

> **JACK WELCH**, *CEO of General Electric, in 2001. In committing GE in the late 1990s to exploiting the Internet's possibilities, Welch came to believe that "the Internet is the Viagra of big business."*

Getting information off the Internet is like taking a drink from a fire hydrant.

> **MITCH KAPOR**, *founder of U.S. software maker Lotus Development, in the late 1990s, on cyber-information overload.*

The Internet is the largest legal creation of wealth in the history of the planet.

> **JOHN DOERR**, *leading Silicon Valley venture capitalist, in the late 1990s. In 2001, after the collapse of hundreds of dot-coms, Doerr apologized for his earlier forecast.*

Let's not get carried away. The information superhighway is a tool, perhaps as revolutionary an innovation as the printing press or the telephone, but a tool nonetheless. A lot of it will be a guy in New Jersey sitting in his room talking to a guy in Iceland about the weather. It will also open up a huge opportunity to waste your time.

> **HAROLD S. GENEEN**, *former CEO of ITT, in his 1997 book,* The Synergy Myth.

I continued to preach the gospel, assuring the unsaved that the Internet was their salvation. But we needed something else to get the world's attention. More marketing bullshit! For a tiny little company with modest but exploding revenues, what was the biggest marketing event of all?

> **JIM CLARK**, *founder of Silicon Graphics and Netscape Communications, in his 2000 memoir* Internet Time: The Making of a Billion-Dollar Start-Up, *on how a successful initial public offering of Netscape shares in 1995 would raise the fledgling company's profile with investors and customers. In the old days, companies became prominent in order to go public; now they went public in order to gain prominence.*

My top ten list of signs that an Internet company's market capitalization is inflated: 10. They have an "e" or an "i" or a "dot-com" as part of their name. 9. Employees' pagers can only receive stock prices. 8. The initial vesting period closed yesterday, and today the office is empty. 7. There are more dogs and cats in their offices than employees. 6. Employees are heard saying, "Profits are so yesterday." 5. The accounts receivable sign hangs over a toilet. 4. The value of the cars in the parking lot exceeds the company's revenue by a factor of four. 3. The investor relations department reports to marketing. 2. Zero revenues, but enough cash to purchase Iceland. 1. Employees ask, "Hey dude, what does the P stand for in P&L?"

> SCOTT McNEALY, *CEO of Sun Microsystems, address at a tech conference in 2000.*

Invective

Rolling in the gutter with a boor would only cause the casual observer to remark, "Look at the two boors wrestling in the gutter"—when in reality there would be a bookseller and a boor.

> LEONARD RIGGIO, *president of U.S. bookseller B. Dalton, in 1988, on why he wouldn't respond to rival Waldenbooks' criticism of his firm's hucksterish TV ads.*

When you're angry, never put it in writing. It's like carving your anger in stone. That makes implacable enemies.

> **ESTÉE LAUDER**, *20th-century U.S. cosmetics magnate, who preferred face-to-face confrontations*

I may be a small company, and you guys may put me out of business. But for every drop of blood I shed, you will shed a barrel.

> **TED TURNER**, *Atlanta broadcast mogul, angry that RCA would not provide a slot on its satellite for his planned CNN cable channel, launched in 1980.*

I'm reminded of something Disraeli once said in Parliament: "Honourable sir, it's true that I am a low, mean snake. But you, sir, could walk beneath me wearing a top hat."

> **RUPERT MURDOCH**, *Australian American media baron, in 1996, on rival media mogul Ted Turner, who had described Murdoch as "the schlockmeister."*

IBM is a perfect partner. Oracle goes out and proclaims you are an idiot. When you alienate everybody, you become someone no one wants to play with.

> **CRAIG CONWAY**, *CEO of U.S. software firm PeopleSoft, who worked at Larry Ellison's Oracle for eight years, in Forbes in 2001 on why he shifted his sales focus to IBM.*

Investing

The way to make money is to buy when blood is running in the streets.

> JOHN D. ROCKEFELLER SR., *U.S. oilman and co-founder in 1862 of the predecessor company to Standard Oil.*

The market is like a beautiful woman—endlessly fascinating, endlessly complex, always changing, always mystifying. I have been absorbed and immersed since 1924 and I know this is no science. It is an art. Now we have computers and all sorts of statistics, but the market is still the same and understanding the market is still no easier. It is personal intuition, sensing patterns of behavior. There is always something unknown, indiscerned.

> EDWARD CROSBY JOHNSON II, *who bought an ailing Fidelity Investments in 1946 and built the Boston firm into a major fund manager, in Adam Smith's,* The Money Game *(1967).*

People are feeling really wounded because they bought stocks at one hundred times revenues, and they can't understand why their life's savings is gone. People, get a grip! Look at what you did! Hey, that truck hit me! Well, if you play in the freeway, you are going to get hit by a truck.

> SCOTT MCNEALY, *CEO of U.S. computer firm Sun Microsystems, in March 2001. Sun's own stock was down to $18.37 at the time, from its fifty-two-week high of $64.68.*

The different investing systems—Ben Graham, growth stocks, and the others—are fine, as long as you have the discipline to stick to them. Most people don't, though, so they have the worst of both worlds. Myself, I have no system. I'm a pragmatist. I just wait until the fourth year, when the economic cycle bottoms, and buy whatever seems attractive at the time, whatever I think will have the biggest bounce.

> **LAURENCE TISCH**, *CEO of U.S. conglomerate Loews, in 1979. Loews's holdings included Loews hotels and theaters, Lorillard tobacco (Kent, Newport, True), and CNA Financial.*

I am not a professional security analyst. I would rather call myself an insecurity analyst.

> **GEORGE SOROS**, *U.S. currency trader, in his 1995 memoir,* Soros on Soros.

I will tell you the secret of getting rich on Wall Street: You try to be greedy when others are fearful and you try to be very fearful when others are greedy.

> **WARREN BUFFETT**, *U.S. investor, in a 1950s lecture on investing.*

If you aren't willing to own a stock for ten years, don't even think about owning it for ten minutes.

> **WARREN BUFFETT**, *CEO of Berkshire Hathaway, in his 1997 letter to shareholders.*

I don't think it's the pathway to long-term success, watching CNBC and checking your account every day. What it leads to is this emotional imbalance that you've created for yourself. If you are sage, you can do that. But if you are an immature investor and you look at it every day, you just become hyper about it.

> CHARLES SCHWAB, *founder of U.S. discount broker Charles Schwab,* in Fast Company *in 2001.*

Law Number XXII: If stock market experts were so expert, they would be buying stock, not selling advice.

> NORMAN AUGUSTINE, *CEO of U.S. defense contractor Martin Marietta and later Lockheed Martin, in* Augustine's Laws *(1986).*

When everyone sees it's a good investment, it's time to sell.

> DAVID H. MURDOCH, *U.S. investment banker whose net worth in 1982 was estimated at $400 million, in the 1980s.*

Investment Banking

Once again, the securities industry is going to the fat farm after having gorged itself in times of plenty. It has happened before and it will happen again.

> GEORGE L. BALL, *CEO of Prudential-Bache Securities, in 1984, on Wall Street layoffs following a market slump.*

The plan at that time most in favor was to start off with the largest possible capitalization and then sell all the stock and all the bonds that could be sold. Whatever money happened to be left over after all the stock and bond-selling expenses and promoters, charges and all that, went grudgingly into the foundation of the business.

> **HENRY FORD**, *founder of Ford Motor, in his 1922 book* My Life and Work, *on the meagre proceeds to the company from raising money in the equity and bond markets.*

The art of investment banking consists of taking a button and making a suit out of it.

> **ANDRÉ MEYER**, *U.S. financier and philanthropist.*

REALITY CHECK

With an evening coat and a white tie, anybody, even a stockbroker, can gain a reputation for being civilized.

> **OSCAR WILDE,** *The Picture of Dorian Gray*

I love the factory. That's what business is all about. Making things. Not this Wall Street stuff, not this lawyer stuff. None of that adds value. You gotta make something.

> **SCOTT MCNEALY**, *CEO of U.S. computer firm Sun Microsystems, in* Fortune *in 1997.*

This one is about two girls who were hiking in the woods. They were crossing a brook when a frog jumped out of the water and said, "Kiss me and I'll turn into an investment banker." One girl promptly picked up the frog and threw him into her knapsack. "Aren't you going to kiss him?" the other girl said. "Are you kidding?" the first one said. "Investment bankers are a dime a dozen. But a talking frog will bring millions."

> **MICHAEL ARMSTRONG**, *CEO of Hughes Electronics and later of AT&T, in a 1995 speech.*

Over a long weekend, I could teach my dog to be an investment banker.

> **HERBERT ALLEN**, *U.S. investment banker at Allen & Co., in the 1980s.*

It's partly the structure of Wall Street, the nature of a boom economy, that you only understand deals when they go wrong.

> **BRUCE WASSERSTEIN**, *U.S. investment banker at Wasserstein Perella & Co., in 2001.*

Leadership

The pressures on a chief executive are all in the direction of hurry-up. But he's also the last person in the company who should lose his patience, or his temper.

> **DONALD N. FREY**, *CEO of Bell & Howell, in* Fortune *in 1976.*

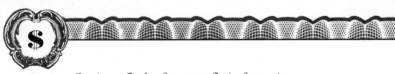

Getting a flock of egos to fly in formation.

> WALTER F. (FREDERICK) LIGHT, *CEO of Brampton, Ontario-based Nortel Networks in the 1980s, on his chief management task.*

I'm infinitely more inclined to lead than push: pushing gets tiresome.

> ROBERT O. ANDERSON, *CEO of U.S. oil giant Atlantic Richfield, in the 1980s.*

[I learned] early that if something went wrong, you should examine what you have done wrong before looking outside yourself for someone to blame. There's the old Army response: "No excuse, sir."

> ROBERT ARTHUR BECK, *appointed CEO of New Jersey-based Prudential Insurance in 1978, and a former member of the 82nd Airborne Division, in Arthur M. Louis's,* The Tycoons *(1981).*

If you're doing it right, you don't feel like you're wielding power.

> ALLEN JACOBSON, *CEO of 3M (formally Minnesota Mining and Manufacturing), in* Forbes *in 1988.*

One of the hardest tasks of leadership is understanding that you are not what you are, but what you're perceived to be by others.

> EDWARD L. FLOM, *CEO of Florida Steel, in a 1987 speech.*

A friend of mine characterizes leaders simply like this: "Leaders don't inflict pain, they bear pain."

> **MAX DEPREE**, *CEO of Herman Miller, a Michigan-based maker of office furniture founded by DePree's father, in his 1989 book* Leadership Is an Art.

We have three hundred tons of brainpower. How can we motivate our people so that those three hundred tons move in a certain direction?

> **GORAN LINDAHL**, *head of Swedish-Swiss engineering firm ABB, in the late 1990s.*

A company is an organic, living, breathing thing, not just an income statement and balance sheet. You have to lead it with that in mind.

> **CARLETON S. (CARLY) FIORINA**, *CEO of Hewlett-Packard, in 2000.*

Management is about persuading people to do things they do not want to do, while leadership is about inspiring people to do things they never thought they could.

> **STEVE JOBS**, *co-founder of Apple Computer, in* EuroBusiness *in 2001.*

Legal Affairs

Gentlemen:

You have undertaken to cheat me. I won't sue you, for the law is too slow. I'll ruin you.

Yours truly,

Cornelius Vanderbilt

> **CORNELIUS VANDERBILT**, *19th-century U.S. financier, to former associates who swindled him out of control of a canal in Nicaragua. Vanderbilt exacted revenge by regaining control of the canal through stock market manipulations that left his adversaries holding worthless shares.*

I don't know as I want a lawyer to tell me what I cannot do. I hire him to tell me how to do what I want to do.

> **JOHN PIERPONT MORGAN**, *U.S. financier and philanthropist, who was prominent in the creation of industrial combines, including U.S. Steel in 1901.*

People started coming around saying that they had a legal problem, but what they really had was a business problem. There is nothing more important to a businessman than to have someone who will solve a problem, particularly someone who will shed some tears with him when he's feeling pain. I built my own clientele [within the company], and it was natural for me to move along as they moved along.

> **IRVING S. (SAUL) SHAPIRO**, *appointed CEO of DuPont in the 1970s after a stint as the firm's head of legal affairs.*

Don't Be Frightened by Your First Lawsuit.

> VICTOR KIAM, *owner of shaving-products maker Remington Products of Bridgeport, Connecticut; chapter title in Kiam's 1986 management primer* Going for It!—How to Succeed as an Entrepreneur.

Luck

With all due respect to Microsoft and Intel, there is no substitute for being in the right place at the right time.

> ANDREW S. GROVE, *CEO of Intel, in* Fortune *in 1993.*

All life's a series of accidents when you're old enough to rationalize your great plan. The idea that I, growing up in Appleton, Wisconsin, would wind up as chairman of Citicorp seemed ridiculous. I never had becoming chairman as a goal; it just happened. Most of it is standin' on the right corner when the bus comes along. And being on the corner with enough experience and smarts that you step on it.

> WALTER WRISTON, *CEO of Citicorp in the 1980s, in* Manhattan, Inc. *in 1985.*

This is amateur sport. The next knock on the door could be Elvis Presley.

> JERRY MOSS, *co-founder of A&M Records, in* Forbes *in 1987.*

Our company has, indeed, *stumbled* onto some of its new products. But never forget that you can only stumble if you're moving.

> RICHARD P. CARLTON, *CEO of 3M, in James C. Collins and Jerry I. Porras's,* Built to Last *(1994).*

When the death rate starts increasing, we don't have to do anything but be a recipient of the windfall.

> ROBERT WALTRIP, *CEO of Service Corp. International, a Houston-based funeral management company, in 1996.*

Work brings money; always plough back; luck may help a man over a ditch—if he jumps well; strive to do a common thing *un*commonly well.

> HENRY JOHN (H. J.) HEINZ, *Pittsburgh-based food magnate who started out as a horseradish producer at age twenty-five in 1869, on maxims for success.*

Managing

The imperfections, that's all I see all day, my own plus everybody else's.

> EDWARD CROSBY (NED) JOHNSON III, *CEO of Fidelity Investments of Boston, the world's largest mutual fund manager.*

Begin with praise and honest appreciation. "A barber lathers a man before he shaves him." ... Talk about your own mistakes before criticizing the other person. ... Let the other man save his face.... Praise the slightest improvement and praise every improvement. Be "hearty" in your approbation and lavish in your praise.... Give a man a fine reputation to live up to.

> **ANDREW CARNEGIE**, *19th-century U.S. steel maker, on "how to change people without giving offense and arousing resentment."*

Well, you know, you don't really do anything different than anybody else does. Mechanically, you read stuff, you answer the phone, you talk to people. That's about all you can do. You write some letters.

> **WILLIAM S. SNEATH**, *CEO of Union Carbide, asked by* Chemical Week *in 1980 about his management style.*

It's of no importance what field an entrepreneur operates in. When I went to Olivetti, I knew absolutely nothing about electronics. Even if I know very little about the food industry, I can say as I take over Buitoni that I've eaten plenty of pasta.

> **CARLO DE BENEDETTI**, *Italian entrepreneur, in the* Wall Street Journal *in 1985.*

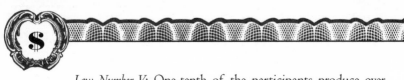

Law Number V: One-tenth of the participants produce over one-third of the output. Increasing the number of participants merely reduces the average output.

> NORMAN R. AUGUSTINE, *CEO of U.S. aerospace firm Martin Marietta, in* Augustine's Laws *(1986).*

I'm a child of the corporate struggle. I spent many years dealing with people trying to do me in. I determined that any operation I ran would be as nonpolitical as I could make it.

> MICHAEL D. EISNER, *CEO of Walt Disney Co., in* Time *in 1988.*

An important mistake I made involved a big computer system project on which we spent nearly two years and maybe $80 million. We tried to do too much at once, and it was a tremendous mistake from which I learned a hell of a lot. I'm not sure that I've learned patience yet, but I've since become a fan of getting away from episodic management—big projects—and toward looking for solutions in decent bite sizes.

> JOHN S. REED, *CEO of Citicorp, in* Forbes *in 1988.*

REALITY CHECK

So much of what we call management consists of making it difficult for people to work.

> PETER DRUCKER, *20th-century management theorist.*

Management means miles. In my case, over four million of them. It is the only way to get to know your people on the ground and in their territory. And it is the only way to get a fact and experience base to make what is without doubt the most important decisions of all—who you promote, who you don't and who you release.... Nothing resonates through an organization faster than who gets promoted and what kind of behavior that promotion signals as being reward. Plato said it long ago: "What is rewarded in a country will be practiced there."

> RICHARD (DICK) CURRIE, *president of George Weston, Canada's largest grocery operator, in 2001.*

The pressure applied by the markets for short-term results is appropriate and fair. On balance, it has made companies more competitive than they would be otherwise. If executives don't want to be subject to market forces, they should go to work for private companies or change professions.

> HARVEY GOLUB, *CEO of American Express, in* Business Week *in 2000. During his seven-year tenure at Amex to that point, the firm's stock had risen in value more than sixfold.*

I expect to spend at least four days a week out of the office meeting employees and customers. More than one day a week in the office, you don't get very much done. You keep holding meetings, and that screws up everybody else's life.

> MICHAEL WALSH, *outgoing CEO of Union Pacific Railroad, in* Fortune *in 1991, on his new responsibilities as CEO of Houston conglomerate Tenneco.*

We are a by-the-book company. It's the only possible way to run a company this size.

> **J. WILLARD (BILL) MARRIOTT JR.,** *CEO of U.S. hotel chain Marriott International, in* Forbes *in 1988. Marriott conceded that as his firm grew to hundreds of thousands of rooms worldwide, local managers could no longer be granted as much autonomy as in Marriott's early days, since confusion and lack of product consistency would result.*

It's kind of like the American politicians who used to visit Vietnam, look around a bit, talk to the top brass in military command, review some statistics, and then proclaim that the war was being won and they could see the light at the end of the tunnel. Right!

> **LARRY BOSSIDY,** *CEO of Honeywell, U.S. electronics firm and defense contractor, with Ram Charan in their 2002 book* Execution: The Discipline of Getting Things Done, *on executives who make a show of visiting far-flung operations, but don't get to the bottom of what's going on.*

Insecure managers create complexity. Frightened, nervous managers use thick, convoluted planning books and busy slides filled with everything they've known since childhood.

> **JACK WELCH,** *CEO of General Electric, in* Harvard Business Review *in 1989.*

Market Research

It is futile to try to measure what people want to read in their newspapers. Most will tell you what they think they want, or should want, to read, but not what they'll actually buy and look at. If such polls reflected reality, there would be a boom in literary supplements.

> RUPERT MURDOCH, *Australian American media baron, in* Forbes *in 1984, deflecting criticism of his sensationalist British tabloids, the* Sun *and* News of the World.

Our plan is to lead the market with new products, rather than ask them what kind of products they want. Instead of doing a lot of market research, we refine a product and try to create a market for it by educating and communicating with the public.

> AKIO MORITA, *CEO of Sony, in his 1986 memoir,* Made in Japan. *Among Sony's products for which there was no demonstrated market were Japan's first magnetic tape recorder (1950), the first all-transistor radio (1955), the first home-use videotape recorder (1964), and the Sony Walkman (1979).*

Since the public does not tell us what it wants, we give it what it ought to have.

> HENRY FORD, *founder of Ford Motor, quoted in the* New York Times Magazine *in 1928.*

There was no market data twenty-five years ago that said the world was demanding microprocessors. I suppose if there were market research before the invention of the steam engine or the light bulb, there wouldn't have been any market data for those either.... I believe in data. But data has its limitations.

ANDREW S. GROVE, *CEO of Intel, in* Report on Business Magazine *in 1996.*

Market Share

Too many people. We must be doing something wrong.

HAROLD ROSS, *founding publisher of the* New Yorker, *on learning that circulation had surpassed three hundred thousand, a number greater than the targeted elite audience—soon after the magazine was launched in 1925.*

Before you can have share of market, you must have share of mind.

LEO BURNETT, *who ran Chicago advertising agency Leo Burnett Co. from 1935 to 1971, speaking to an audience of ad executives in 1955. Burnett's solution was to create memorable characters such as the Marlboro Man for Philip Morris Cos. and Tony the Tiger for Kellogg Co.*

Volume times zero isn't too healthy.

LEE IACOCCA, *president of Ford Motor, in* Newsweek *in 1971, on the perils of easy financing to capture market share.*

The next guy who talks to me about tonnage is going to get his salary in tons, and we'll see how he converts that into dollars.

> **JOHN C. LOBB**, *president of Crucible Steel and later of Northern Electric, in the* New York Times *in 1967, on the perils of discount pricing to capture market share.*

If I hear anybody talking about how big their share of the market is or what they're trying to do to increase their share of the market, I'm going to personally see that a black mark gets put in their personnel folder.

> **DAVID PACKARD**, *co-founder of Hewlett-Packard, in a 1974 meeting with managers, on the perils of capturing market share with elaborate marketing campaigns.*

The soft drink industry in the 1980s tended toward the mindless pursuit of market share. Managing share without profit is like breathing air without oxygen. It feels okay for a while, but in the end it kills you.

> **ROGER A. ENRICO**, *CEO of PepsiCo Worldwide Beverages, in* Fortune *in 1990.*

Marketing

The changes in new [car] models should be so novel and attractive as to create dissatisfaction with past models. The laws of Paris dressmakers have come to be a factor in the automobile industry.

> **ALFRED P. (PRITCHARD) SLOAN JR.**, *CEO of General Motors, in 1922, introducing the era of planned obsolescence.*

Wine is the temperate, civilized, sacred, romantic mealtime beverage recommended in the Bible and praised for centuries by statesmen, philosophers, poets, and scholars.

> **ROBERT MONDAVI**, *founder of California's Robert Mondavi Winery and a tireless promoter of Napa Valley. His great triumph was to see Baron Philippe de Rothschild take back his 1973 assertion that California wine "all comes out industrially uniform, like Coca-Cola."*

If fashion isn't worn by everybody, then it is only eccentricity.

> **GABRIELLE (COCO) CHANEL**, *French couturier, in Edmonde Charles-Roux's*, Chanel *(1975).*

We sell hope.

> **CHARLES REVSON**, *co-founder of U.S. cosmetics giant Revlon, frequent aphorism. Andrew Tobias, in his Revson biography* Fire and Ice *(1975), quotes an admiring associate who said Revson "lent women a little immoral support."*

We're not selling watches to tell the time. We're selling them to people who belong to a certain social class, who want to show off.

> **DOMINIQUE PERRIN**, *president of luxury goods marketer Cartier, in 1987.*

I must keep telling my marketing people not to make the beer bottle too elaborate with gold foil or fancy labels. Otherwise, the housewife will be too intimidated to take it off the supermarket shelf.

> **ALFRED HENRY (FREDDY) HEINEKEN**, *CEO of Dutch brewer Heineken from 1963 to 1989.*

It costs a lot of money for us to make our places look cheap.

> **JIM SINEGAL**, *CEO of U.S. discount warehouse operator Price Costco, in the 1990s.*

We're in the business of selling pleasure. We don't sell handbags or haute couture. We sell dreams.

> **ALAIN WERTHEIMER**, *chairman of French fashion house Chanel, interviewed in* Wine Spectator *in the 1990s.*

We figured that a customer base with a salary was better than a customer base with an allowance.

> **MICHAEL WEISS**, *president of U.S. retailer Express, on the decision by his women's wear chain to target an older audience, in the 1990s.*

Ice cream is the rock 'n' roll of food. It completely bypasses the intellect.

> **HART MELVIN**, *co-owner of Toronto-based ice-cream maker Gelato Fresco, in* Report on Business Magazine *in 1992.*

This fishing tackle manufacturer I knew had all these flashy green and purple lures. I asked, "Do fish take these?" "Charlie," he said, "I don't sell these lures to fish."

> **CHARLES T. MUNGER**, *partner with Warren Buffett in U.S. investment firm Berkshire Hathaway, in 1993.*

There is usually only one thought going through the mind of a bereaved family when they walk through the doors of a funeral home...*get me out of here.* Of course, every funeral director knows this. Which is why the most expensive merchandise is always brought to their attention first—and why, for example, the less expensive caskets are always shown in the ugliest colors.

> **JIM ST. GEORGE**, *CEO of coffin maker Consumer-Casket USA, in* Harper's *in 1997.*

You've got to evangelize the concept.

> **JOHN T. CHAMBERS**, *CEO of Cisco Systems, often criticized by rivals in the late 1990s for "Elmer Gantry" excesses in exhorting potential customers to embrace the Internet or risk becoming roadkill on the Information Superhighway.*

I believe in what I'm doing. The fact the chairman gets out there and talks about his own products and makes a fool of himself occasionally helps.

> SIR RICHARD BRANSON, *CEO of British conglomerate Virgin Group, in 2000.*

We're not in the soft drink business. We are in the fashion business. It is a constant whirl of new products, flavors, and packaging, pitched to consumers who want the latest thing.

> MICHAEL WEINSTEIN, *CEO of soft-drink maker Snapple, in 2001.*

I grew to see that everything for sale on the fashion floors at Macy's could enlarge a woman's life if I created an idea, a drama for it. That, I realized, is what fashion advertising and marketing are supposed to do—enlarge someone's life through her or his imagination.

> MARY WELLS LAWRENCE, *co-founder in 1966 of New York advertising agency Wells Rich Greene, in her 2002 memoir,* A Big Life in Advertising. *Wells Lawrence started out as a copywriter for McKelvey's department store in her native Youngstown, Ohio, later moving to Bambergers in Newark, New Jersey, and McCreery's and Macy's in Manhattan.*

Mea Culpas

My life is a war between the forces of good and evil.

>TED TURNER, *U.S. media mogul, who was kicked out of Brown and drank his way through the America's Cup competition, but managed to win the yacht race and launch CNN in 1980. By his own frequent admission, Turner swung from moments of kindhearted brilliance to boorish stupidity.*

If there's going to be a burning at the stake, you might as well rope me up as well.

>BEN F. LOVE, *chairman of Texas Commerce Bancshares, in 1985, after announcing its first profit decline ever.*

I'm the first to admit that our timing couldn't have been worse. But I take comfort in one fact: the last guy who was perfect in this world was crucified two thousand years ago.

>CEDRIC RITCHIE, *CEO of Bank of Nova Scotia, on the bank's purchase of investment dealer McLeod Young Weir just before the October 1987 stock market crash.*

In statements I made for an article in your July 19 issue ("I still think they're idiots"), I am guilty of a breach of etiquette as I labeled my adversaries rather than their conduct. For this I must apologize to the partners of the Lodestar Group. What I should have said is that I found their proposals to be idiotic.

>CHARLES M. DENNY JR., *chairman of ADC Telecommunications of Minneapolis, in a 1993 letter to* Forbes.

The decision went beyond dumb and reached all the way out to stupid.

> **LEE IACOCCA**, *CEO of Chrysler, in 1987, on his company having sold cars that had been damaged during testing as new cars.*

We follow public taste more than we lead it, which is nothing to boast about.

> **RUPERT MURDOCH**, *Australian American media baron, in a Yale University lecture in the late 1990s.*

REALITY CHECK

Always acknowledge a fault frankly. This will throw those in authority off their guard and give you an opportunity to commit more.

MARK TWAIN

For one of our tobacco companies to commission this study was not just a terrible mistake, it was wrong and I sincerely regret this extraordinarily unfortunate incident.

> **GEOFFREY BIBLE**, *CEO of U.S. tobacco giant Philip Morris, in 2001, apologizing for a report released by the firm's Czech affiliate that said smokers are good for the country because they die more quickly, easing the pension burden.*

We were hoping to build a small, profitable company. And of course, what we've done is build a large, unprofitable company.

JEFF BEZOS, *founder and CEO of Amazon.com, a U.S. online retailer that by 2002, after seven years in business, had yet to record an annual profit.*

In some ways I'm glad for this early near-disaster in our company's history. It quickly taught us that we were not invincible. Perhaps the only way to inoculate against arrogance is experiencing a setback that sticks in the collective memory. Perhaps we can rename 2001 the Year of Arrogance Revealed.

DONNA DUBINSKY, *co-founder and CEO of Handspring, a leading U.S. maker of paging devices, in* Forbes ASAP *in 2002, recalling early mistakes at Handspring, including the lack of a distribution channel, reliance on online sales when the Web was not ready for prime time, and chronic late shipments.*

I violated the Noah rule: Predicting rain doesn't count; building arks does.

WARREN BUFFETT, *CEO of Berkshire Hathaway, in a 2001 letter to shareholders, on the firm's failure to build adequate reserves against the possibility of severe underwriting losses. In previous years, Buffett had repeatedly warned of the high risks inherent in the "super-cat," or super-catastrophe insurance business.*

Media Relations

I'm content to have people think I live in a cave and wear horns.

> **ELEANOR MCCLATCHY**, *reclusive proprietor of the McClatchy newspaper dynasty founded by grandfather, James McClatchy, who launched the* Sacramento Bee *in 1857.*

I find it embarrassing to have to explain to a journalist things I don't understand myself.

> **ALFRED P. (PRITCHARD) SLOAN**, *CEO of General Motors for twenty-three years, beginning in 1923, on why he hired one of the first public-relations executives in the United States at GM.*

I am certain anything favorable you might write about me would only give the Communistic yellow press another opportunity to vilify and lie about me.

> **SIR HERBERT HOLT**, *Canadian financier and philanthropist, in 1938, to a* Toronto Daily Star *newspaper reporter requesting an interview.*

I don't owe money to the banks. I'm not running for office. I'm not a public company. I don't give a damn what anybody says. I'm going to do what I think is right. Not many people have that luxury.

> **SIR JAMES GOLDSMITH**, *British corporate raider, in 1979. The litigious tycoon* did *care enough about what was said about him to successfully sue British gossip magazine* Private Eye *for libel in the 1980s.*

Never complain, never explain.

> **HENRY FORD II**, *chairman of Ford Motor in the 1960s and 1970s. Ford's most famous aphorism was borrowed from Benjamin Disraeli, the 19th-century British prime minister.*

And when, may I ask, was the last time you were in a Turkish whorehouse?

> **W. EARLE McLAUGHLIN**, *CEO of Royal Bank of Canada in the 1960s and 1970s, to business chronicler Peter C. Newman, who had described the overblown décor of the bank's new Toronto head office.*

There is always a certain—call it a hazard if you will—in being in the public eye and being on the record, because you—we all—can put our foot in the mouth. And I guess I can do it as well as anybody.

> **THOMAS A. MURPHY**, *CEO of General Motors, in Arthur M. Louis*, The Tycoons *(1981).*

REALITY CHECK

My pappy told me never to bet my bladder against a brewery or get into an argument with people who buy ink by the barrel.

> **LANE KIRKLAND,** *U.S. labor leader.*

No two-bit writer from the *New York Times* is going to diminish my sense of accomplishment.

> **DAVID RICKEY**, *CEO of Applied Micro Circuits, in 2001, after a series of* Times *articles casting doubt on AMC's prospects.*

How the fuck can you get $495 for your newsletter when it's clear you have no fucking idea what you're talking about?

> **BILL GATES**, *co-founder of Microsoft, in an exchange at a 1991 investors forum with industry newsletter writer Stewart Alsop, who had just criticized a recently unveiled Microsoft product.*

After creating such a sensation, I do not think it would be proper for me to say the punishment was too severe. All the criticism in the press taught me many things about myself I could not see before.

> **HIROTOMO TAKEI**, *Japanese conglomerate owner, in 1992, after being ordered to serve four years in prison for evading $27 million in taxes.*

I hope we go back to a model where the product that we're selling is the product that the company makes, whatever it is, as opposed to the CEO, the brand, the executives, the shareholders, whatever. Because ultimately the stock price—I learned this sort of the hard way—the stock price is the tail of the dog.

> **ERIC E. SCHMIDT**, *CEO of U.S. software firm Novell and later of Internet search engine Google, in the* New York Times *in 2001, despairing of the 1990s media fixation with CEOs at the expense of a firm's products.*

It's always dangerous to give interviews.

STEVE JOBS, *announcing the sale of his computer firm, Next, to Apple Computer at a press conference where it was pointed out he had recently dismissed Apple as being dead in the water; quoted in the* Wall Street Journal *in 1996.*

The socially mobile are portrayed as uncaring, businessmen as crooks. Moneymaking is to be despised.

RUPERT MURDOCH, *Australian American media baron, in 1989.*

I shudder when businesspeople claim they've been sandbagged by the press. Quite frankly, if you can be entrapped or tripped up by a reporter, maybe you deserve it.

ADAM ZIMMERMAN, *CEO of Toronto-based Noranda Forest, in his 1997 memoir,* Who's in Charge Here, Anyway?

When bad news becomes water torture—bad news followed by bad news by bad news—that's when CEOs lose credibility.

DENNIS KOZLOWSKI, *CEO of U.S. conglomerate Tyco International, in 2001, on the need to get all the bad news out at once. Kozlowski quit the firm a year later after his arrest on charges of evading sales tax on art purchases. Tyco was under investigation for dubious accounting practices at the time.*

You wouldn't say it's harsh if you were in the tabloids all the time.

OPRAH WINFREY, *majority owner of Chicago-based entertainment firm Harpo, in* Fortune *in 2002, on why her employees are required to sign a lifelong confidentiality agreement.*

Memos, Reports, and Meetings

I don't believe I've ever used such terms with you as "idiotic." I may have *thought* your excessive takes and angles were idiotic, but the most I've said was that they were a waste of my personal money.

> DAVID O. SELZNICK, *who in 1936 founded Selznick International Pictures, in a memo responding to a protest from director Charles Vidor. Selznick used memos to manage his studio. Director Alfred Hitchcock said in 1965, "When I came to America twenty-five years ago to direct* Rebecca, *David Selznick sent me a memo. [pause] I've just finished reading it. [pause] I think I may turn it into a motion picture. [pause] I plan to call it* The Longest Story Ever Told."

There aren't any categories of problems here. There's just one problem. Some of us aren't paying enough attention to our customers.

> THOMAS J. WATSON SR., *founder of IBM. Watson made the comment after enduring a lengthy discussion among top managers about problems in customer relations, at which point he strode to the front of the room, with a sweep of his arm sent a pile of reports flying off a table, made his comment, then walked out of the room. Recounted by a witness in Thomas J. Peters and Robert H. Waterman Jr.'s,* In Search of Excellence: Lessons from America's Best-Run Companies *(1982).*

A conference can provide an effective channel of communication, but too often the procedures tend either to become too formalized or to degenerate into a Babel of demogagic pronouncements or interminable rambling. In Japan, where decision making by consensus is the rule, staff meetings are particularly trying; they can go on for hours without getting anywhere.

KONOSUKE MATSUSHITA, *founder of Matsushita Electric Industrial, maker of Panasonic, Technics, and Quasar products, in the 1970s.*

REALITY CHECK

Every memorandum will leak. Every memorandum marked "confidential" will leak even faster.

ROBERT REICH, *economist and U.S. labor secretary.*

I can get a division manager to cough up a seventy-page proposal overnight. What I don't seem to be able to do is get a one-page analysis...[that] says, "Here are the three reasons it might be better; here are the three things that might make it worse."

B. CHARLES AMES, *CEO of Reliance Electric, a leading U.S. maker of electric equipment. Cited in Thomas J. Peters and Robert H. Waterman Jr.'s,* In Search of Excellence: Lessons from America's Best-Run Companies *(1982).*

It's estimated that the dollar cost of a manager's time, including overhead allotted to it, is around $100 per hour. A meeting attended by ten managers for two hours thus costs the company $2,000. Most expenditures of $2,000—such as buying a copying machine or making a transatlantic trip—have to be approved in advance by senior people, yet a manager can call a meeting and commit $2,000 worth of managerial resources on a whim. If that meeting is unnecessary or so poorly run that it achieves nothing, that's $2,000 wasted.

> ANDREW S. GROVE, *president of Intel, in a 1983 essay in* Fortune, *"How (and Why) to Run a Meeting."*

There's no substitute for face-to-face. Something happens when you are in the room with people with whom you work, trying to solve a problem together by just listening to them. And the email becomes more meaningful after the trip with the face-to-face.

> SHELLY LAZARUS, *CEO of U.S. advertising firm Ogilvy & Mather, interviewed in the* New York Times *in 1999.*

Mergers and Acquisitions

Price of *Herald* three cents daily. Five cents Sunday. Bennett.

> JAMES GORDON BENNETT, *19th-century U.S. newspaper publisher, telegraphed reply to rival William Randolph Hearst's inquiry about the cost of acquiring Bennett's New York Herald.*

She asked for a fashion magazine and I went out and got her *Vogue.*

> **SAMUEL IRVING (S. I.) NEWHOUSE,** *referring to his wife, said to be his rationale for building his Condé Nast stable of magazines.*

We'd do nothing for six months, while we put the ferrets in.

> **SIR JAMES HANSON,** *later Lord Hanson, British corporate raider prominent in the 1980s, whose first step after acquiring a firm was to identify assets to be sold and costs to be cut.*

It was more than I would like to have spent, but I was in a poker game and couldn't see the other players.

> **GEORGE KELLER,** *CEO of Standard Oil of California (later Chevron), about his firm's $13.2 billion acquisition of Gulf Oil, in* Time *in 1984.*

Every single guy thought about sleeping with every single girl, and all possibilities were examined, and it almost never happened.

> **MITCH KAPOR,** *founder of U.S. software maker Lotus Development, in the early 1990s, drawing an analogy between his days as a Yale undergraduate and the paucity of mergers among software companies.*

What did I know about MTV? I only knew I couldn't stand looking at it.

> **SUMNER REDSTONE,** *controlling shareholder of media conglomerate Viacom, on its purchase of music-video channel MTV, in the late 1990s.*

Any dope with a checkbook can buy a company. It's what you do afterward that matters.

> **HENRY SILVERMAN**, *founder of franchising firm HFS, in* Fortune *in 1997. HFS subsequently acquired CUC International in a botched merger that nearly destroyed the combined firm, renamed Cendant.*

In most mergers, two people stand up, they high-five, they say "this is the greatest thing. We're going to have all these synergies." And you know it just can't be that great, and then a year later one of the two is gone and things haven't quite worked out. In this case, I have to say, and this is not an arrogant statement, the concept of putting these two companies together is profound. It's a revolutionary change.

> **GERALD M. LEVIN**, *CEO of AOL Time Warner, in a 2000* Business Week *interview on the combination of America Online and Time Warner. Two years later, Levin had quit and AOL Time Warner wrote off $54 billion in goodwill, acknowledging the overvalued price of the merger.*

Mission

What a marvelous opportunity for attacking the devil!

> **W. T. STEAD**, *on taking control of the* Northern Echo, *England's first halfpenny daily, in 1871. Stead, a spiritualist, went down with the* Titanic.

I will construct the best cars at the lowest prices, so that one day every family in France can have its own little car.

LOUIS RENAULT, *French automaker, upon visiting Henry Ford's factory in Dearborn, Michigan, in 1911 to study mass-production techniques.*

If America is not to go the way the way of Europe, the mass of the people must realize their economic stake in our present system, must find in it the opportunity and emotional outlet that people abroad think they see in the socialist state.

CHARLES EDWARD MERRILL, *founder in 1940 of brokerage Merrill Lynch, which popularized Main Street investing.*

We are polishing the floors and furniture, cleaning the rug, killing the bugs, sweetening the air, and waxing the old man's car. And whenever you get bit by a mosquito, remember I'm smiling.

SAMUEL CURTIS JOHNSON, *fourth-generation head of family-controlled Johnson Wax, who took over the firm in 1967.*

I told the guys they ought to design a calculator to fit in my shirt pocket, so they came and measured my pocket.

WILLIAM (BILL) HEWLETT, *co-founder of Hewlett-Packard, recalling the advent of HP's first handheld scientific calculators in 1972, which were destined to make the slide rule obsolete.*

I happened on the idea of fitting an engine to a bicycle simply because I did not want to ride crowded trains and buses.

SOICHIRO HONDA, *founder of Honda, in* Motorcyclist *in 1988.*

Barring satellite problems, we won't be signing off until the world ends. We'll be on, and we will cover the end of the world, live, and that will be our last event. We'll play the National Anthem only one time, on the first of June [the scheduled starting date], and when the end of the world comes we'll play "Nearer My God to Thee" before we sign off.

> TED TURNER, *media mogul, announcing the launch in 1980 of CNN, the first all-news TV channel.*

I founded Wang Laboratories to show that Chinese could excel at things other than running laundries and restaurants.

> AN WANG, *whose Wang Laboratories, a Massachusetts-based computer maker, flourished in the 1970s, but had gone into irreversible steep decline by the late 1980s.*

We deal with warmth, affection, friendship, and love. That's nicer than selling napalm.

> RUSSELL BERRIE, *who launched toy maker Russ Berrie & Co. in a rented garage in 1963. His estimated net worth in 1985 was $180 million.*

I'm trying to be the bridge from what Walt Disney made and created to whoever will be the next person after me that maintains that same philosophy of, "Let's put on a show." Let's be silly. We're a silly company. Let's never not be a silly company.

> MICHAEL D. EISNER, *CEO of Walt Disney Co., in the* New York Times *in 2001.*

Our motto was, "Shameless exploitation in pursuit of the common good."

> **PAUL NEWMAN**, *actor and founder of Newman's Own line of food products, the profits from which he donated to charity, in the 1990s.*

Basically gum is an adult pacifier.

> **WILLIAM WRIGLEY**, *grandson of candy company founder William Wrigley Jr., in* Forbes *in 1988.*

I felt we could change the whole function of the bathroom and make it stimulating, possibly even social.

> **HERB KOHLER JR.**, *CEO of Wisconsin-based Kohler, a maker of bathroom fixtures, and grandson of the founder.*

Our goal is world domination, just like Microsoft.

> **NAVEEN JAIN**, *CEO of Internet start-up InfoSpace and a former employee of Microsoft, in the 1990s.*

Oh, well, the reason we're doing software here at Oracle is because...what I really care about is making the world a better place.... [Makes gagging sound.] People say this and get away with it. I can't deal with the fog of deceit.

> **LARRY ELLISON**, *co-founder and CEO of U.S. software firm Oracle, in Mark Leibovich's,* The New Imperialists *(2002), showing disdain for rival high-tech CEOs who declare their mission to be to save the world rather than to become fabulously rich.*

Mistakes

I should have just said, now Bill, you set the price, and I'll take it. That's what I should have done, and I've always regretted that we didn't get together. I consider it one of the biggest mistakes I've ever made. Gates has never kidded me about that, but I think if the shoe were on the other foot, I'd probably needle him.

> **H. ROSS PEROT**, *CEO of Electronic Data Systems (EDS), recalling an opportunity to buy the four-year-old Microsoft in 1979 in a deal that collapsed when Gates held out for what Perot considered too high a price—somewhere between $40 million and $50 million. (In 2000, Microsoft's market value exceeded $500 billion.)*

I can tolerate one or two mistakes, then I'll cut their hearts out with a spoon.

> **KATHERINE HAMMER**, *CEO of Evolutionary Technologies International, on dealings with her research scientists, in the late 1990s.*

REALITY CHECK

There is no mistake; there has been no mistake; and there shall be no mistake.

ARTHUR WELLESLEY, *1st Duke of Wellington*

Being in the microcomputer business is like going fifty-five miles an hour three feet from a cliff. If you make the wrong turn, you're bankrupt so fast you don't know what hit you.

> **GEORGE MORROW,** *CEO of the recently bankrupt microcomputer maker Morrow, in 1986.*

Once the corporate ethos is that the corporation cannot have made a mistake, then it's going to go farther and father off course. The CEO becomes a bit like a pilot on an aircraft who says to the altimeter, "What's the height?" and hears the altimeter reply, "What would you like it to be?"

> **JOHN CLEESE,** *co-founder of Monty Python's Flying Circus and founder of an executive-training company, in the 1990s.*

New Coke was the smallest mistake in history. After New Coke failed, [Coca-Cola chief executive Roberto Goizueta] knew he had no choice. There could never be a "new improved" product. The product was untouchable.... Roberto Goizueta lived to see the *Guinness Book of World Records* list Coca-Cola as the most powerful brand.

> **BARRY J. GIBBONS,** *CEO of Burger King in the early 1990s, in his 2002 book,* Dream Merchants & Howboys: Mavericks, Nutters, and the Road to Business Success.

Monopoly

The Standard was an angel of mercy, reaching down from the sky, and saying, "Get into the ark. Put in your old junk. We'll take all the risks!"

> **JOHN D. ROCKEFELLER SR.**, *co-founder in 1862 of the predecessor company to Standard Oil, on his practice of forcing smaller rivals to sell out to him or be crushed by his Standard Oil trusts. Cited in H.W. Brands's,* Masters of Enterprise *(1999).*

I found that competition was supposed to be a menace, and that a good manager circumvented his competitors by getting a monopoly by artificial means.

> **HENRY FORD**, *founder of Ford Motor, in his 1922 memoir,* My Life and Work, *disparaging rivals who were more zealous about achieving market dominance than product innovation.*

We don't want most of the business; we want it all.

> **ERNEST GALLO**, *co-founder of E. & J. Gallo Winery, in the* New York Times *in 1997.*

My whole focus is, how can I get a monopoly?

> **SAMUEL ZELL**, *leading U.S. real estate developer based in Chicago, in the 1980s.*

At heart, all of us are monopolists.

> **PETER GODSOE**, *CEO of Bank of Nova Scotia, in 1998, on merger plans among Canada's "Big Five" banks.*

The heroic role of the captain of industry is that of a deliverer from an excess of business management. It is a casting out of businessmen by the chief businessman.

> **THORSTEIN VEBLEN,** *The Theory of Business Enterprise* (1904)

We want to monopolize the software business.

> **BILL GATES,** *co-founder of Microsoft, a frequent comment in the 1970s before his firm had a PR and legal staff to discourage such candid articulations of his mission.*

Do you see people coming in here at 9:30 in the morning, putting their feet up, wondering what they are going to do, as a monopolist would? We're just trying to stay even with the industry and we are working like the dickens to do it.

> **JOHN F. AKERS,** *incoming CEO of IBM, in 1985, on longstanding allegations that his firm controlled the computing industry. In fact, IBM was at that point losing its briefly held control of the newly emerging PC industry, a fate that would help trigger Akers's ouster as CEO in the 1990s.*

I don't mean to sound egomaniacal, but Perry Como used to own Christmas on TV. By "own," I mean monopolize and influence.

> **MARTHA STEWART,** *CEO of Martha Stewart Omnimedia, in the 1990s, on her goals for the company.*

Paranoia

I seldom put my head upon the pillow at night without speaking a few words to myself in this way: "Now a little success, soon you will fall down, soon you will be overthrown. Because you have got a start, you think you are quite a merchant; look out, or you will lose your head—go steady."

> JOHN D. ROCKEFELLER SR., *U.S. industrialist and founder of Standard Oil, in his autobiography, recalling his cautious regard of success while in his twenties.*

I think we need to be paranoid optimists.

> ROBERT J. EATON, *CEO of Chrysler, in a 1997 speech, midway between the crises of the early 1990s and 2001–2002 that nearly crippled the firm.*

Everything we touched in those first years of Wells Rich Greene set some kind of record. We never fell into the trap of believing our fortunes couldn't change, though; we ran scared a lot of the time; we used to describe those days as living in a tank full of jellyfish, we kept expecting the sting. It was too good to be true, too good to last.

> MARY WELLS LAWRENCE, *co-founder in 1966 of New York advertising agency Wells Rich Greene, in 2002. WRG was one of the hottest shops on Madison Avenue in the late 1960s and early 1970s, with award-winning campaigns for Braniff International, Alka Seltzer, Benson & Hedges 100s and New York State ("I Love New York"), but its popularity had cooled off by the time Wells Lawrence sold the firm to a French agency in 1990.*

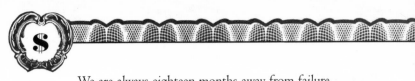

We are always eighteen months away from failure.

> **BILL GATES**, *co-founder of Microsoft, on the need for constant innovation in products and marketing, in the 1980s.*

Part of my job is to keep a vague sense of unease percolating through the entire company. The minute you say the job is done, you're dead.

> **ARTHUR MARTINEZ**, *CEO of Sears Roebuck & Co.*, in Business Week *in 1994.*

Only the paranoid survive.

> **ANDREW S. GROVE**, *CEO of Intel*, in Fortune *in 1995. Grove subsequently used the expression as the title for his memoir.*

I go to sleep worrying someone's going to leave cleat marks on my face before I wake up.

> **CANDICE CARPENTER**, *founder of Internet firm iVillage, in the late 1990s.*

We have a healthy paranoia that makes Andy Grove look relaxed. Any company that thinks it's utterly unbeatable is already beaten. So when I begin to think we're getting a little bit too confident, you'll see me emphasizing the paranoia side. And then when I feel that there's a little bit too much fear and apprehension, I'll just jump back to the other side. My job is to keep those scales perfectly balanced.

> **JOHN T. CHAMBERS**, *CEO of Cisco Systems*, in Fast Company *in 2001.*

Perquisites

I don't ride the subway. I grew up on the subway. I know what it's like. I'm not going to wear sackcloth and ashes about it. Most of us who spent time standing around on Army chow lines vowed that we weren't going to do it in the future, and I haven't.

> DAVID MAHONEY, *CEO of U.S. conglomerate Norton Simon, who started out as a mailroom clerk at a New York ad agency, responding to criticism for having a company jet—a rare perk in the 1970s.*

When I was twenty-seven I was driving my own Rolls-Royce. Today it may be owned by Hanson, but the point is I don't need the company to keep me in the style in which I have lived for years.

> SIR JAMES HANSON, *founder of British conglomerate Hanson PLC, responding to criticism in the 1980s about his corporate perks.*

A tremendous amount of business is discussed at activities like this. [It] isn't all just discussing how pretty the bride looks.

> STANFORD C. STODDARD, *former CEO of Michigan National, a major banking firm, in 1986, explaining to a judge why he invoiced his employer for the orchestra at his daughter's wedding reception.*

All these planes give my CEOs something to aspire to.

> KENNETH LAY, *chairman of U.S. energy trader Enron, in a 2001 interview a few months before the company's bankruptcy, on his use of the "Enron Air Force" to incentivize executives.*

My philosophy, policy, and style always have been that first class costs only a few dollars more and is a smart investment for a smart company on the climb.

> **AL NEUHARTH**, *former CEO of Gannett, in his 1989 memoir,* Confessions of an S.O.B., *in which he includes an angry memo to Gannett's director of flight operations about the lack of hot water for the shower in the company's Gulfstream.*

I only flew Concorde three times, and they were all special offers.

> **KAJSA LEANDER**, *co-founder of Boo.com, an ill-fated European online fashion vendor done in by extravagant start-up expenses, in 2002.*

Philanthropy

The man who dies leaving behind him millions of available wealth, which was his to administer during life, will pass away "unwept, unhonored, and unsung," no matter to what uses he leaves the dross which he cannot take with him. Of such as these the public verdict will then be: "The man who dies thus rich dies disgraced."

> **ANDREW CARNEGIE**, *pioneering U.S. steel maker, in his 1889 essay* "Wealth." *Carnegie donated about $350 million in his lifetime, or 90 percent of his fortune.*

I decided to make the orphan boys of the United States my heirs. The biggest influence in a boy's life is what his dad does; and, when a boy doesn't happen to have any sort of dad, he is a special mark for destiny. I am afraid that most of our orphan boys have a bad time of it and that many never have a chance. Well, I am going to give some of them a chance my way.

MILTON SNAVELY HERSHEY, *founder in 1894 of Hershey Foods, whose donation of his stake in the company to a school for orphaned boys that he built in the company town of Hershey, Pennsylvania, accounts for Hershey Foods' current status as the world's largest firm controlled by an orphanage.*

About the year 1890 I was still following the haphazard fashion of giving here and there as appeals presented themselves. I investigated as I could, and worked myself almost to a nervous breakdown in groping my way, without sufficient guide or chart, through this ever-widening field of philanthropic endeavor.

JOHN D. ROCKEFELLER SR., *U.S. oil baron who suffered nervous disorders until he developed a methodical strategy for donating money, in the early 20th century.*

Hell, why should a man pile up a lot of goddamned money for somebody else to spend after he's gone?

A. P. (AMADEO PETER) GIANNINI (1870–1949), *founder of Bank of America, when he realized toward the end of his life that he was worth almost a million dollars—and promptly gave half of it away.*

REALITY CHECK

Cain took care not to commit another murder, unlike our railway shareholders (I am one) who kill and maim shunters by hundreds to save the cost of automatic couplings, and make atonement by annual subscriptions to deserving causes.

> **GEORGE BERNARD SHAW,** *preface to an edition of his play*
> Major Barbara

They don't put luggage racks on hearses.

> **ROBERT HENRY DEDMAN,** *Dallas resort developer, in 1988, on plans to donate at least a third of his $600 million fortune while he was alive rather than leave it to a charitable trust.*

The mothers are going to walk right up to that computer and say, "My children are dying, what can you do?" They're not going to sit there and like, browse eBay or something. What they want is for their children to live. They don't want their children's growth to be stunted. Do you really have to put in computers to figure that out?

> **BILL GATES,** *co-founder of Microsoft, at a 2001 conference on bringing the Internet revolution to the developing world. Gates doubted the value of donating a computer to an African village. "Do people have a clear view of what it means to live on one dollar a day?" he said. "There is no electricity in that house. None."*

I am not the Salvation Army.

> **ROBERT MAXWELL**, *British press lord, in* Time *in 1988, on his attitude toward corporate philanthropy.*

I keep hearing, "Feed the poor, clothe the hungry, give shelter to those who don't have it." The bozos that say this don't recognize that capitalism and technology have done more to feed and clothe and shelter and heal people than all the charity and church programs in history. So they preach about it, and we are the ones doing it. They rob Peter to pay Paul, but they always forget that Peter is the one that is creating the wealth in the first place.

> **T. J. RODGERS**, *CEO of U.S.-based Cypress Semiconductor, in 2001.*

Posterity

THE FINAL CONDENSATION.

> *Grave marker inscription selected by* **DEWITT WALLACE**, *co-founder in 1922 of* Reader's Digest *magazine.*

Oh, let the fairy tales continue. Who gives a damn?

> **HENRY FORD II**, *CEO of Ford Motor from 1960 to 1979, when a biographer told him that his book would give Ford the chance to set the record straight about the auto czar's life.*

I didn't want to do schoolroom additions. I wanted to leave footprints in the sand.

> **JOHN CALVIN PORTMAN,** *20th-century U.S. architect and developer, noted for pioneering skyscraper hotels with soaring atria in the 1970s.*

Composers are remembered by posterity while businessmen are forgotten.

> **GORDON GETTY,** *U.S. oil scion and music composer, in* Life *in 1989.*

Why would we? It's a bunch of junk.

> **WILLIAM (BILL) HEWLETT,** *asked on the fiftieth birthday of Hewlett-Packard if he and co-founder Dave Packard would buy the famous Palo Alto, California, garage in which they launched HP with a $539 grubstake in 1939. (Under a later generation of managers, HP bought and restored the garage, which is a designated California State landmark.)*

You will leave no heritage for your children. Your name will be forgotten. You will fail. You will fail in everything you do.

> **ANDREW S. GROVE,** *CEO of Intel, cited in* Slate *in 1997, on the folly of dwelling on one's legacy.*

Who the hell cares? The day you retire, you're finished. The day you die, you're dead.

> **WILLIAM JOVANOVICH,** *CEO of book publisher Harcourt Brace Jovanovich, in* Forbes *in 1997, when asked how he would like to go down in history.*

Predictions

You can't get people to sit over an explosion.

> ALBERT A. POPE, *thriving bicycle manufacturer who went into the automobile business, in 1900, skeptical about the potential of the internal combustion engine.*

Who the hell wants to hear actors talk?

> HARRY M. WARNER, *president of Warner Bros. studio, circa 1927. Yet it was Warner Bros. that released the first "talkie,"* The Jazz Singer, *that same year.*

I see no reason for the end-of-the-year slump which some people are predicting.

> CHARLES MITCHELL, *CEO of National City Bank, forerunner of Citibank, and a director of the New York Federal Reserve Bank, two weeks prior to the great market crash of October 29, 1929.*

Those who voluntarily sell stocks at current prices are extremely foolish.

> OWEN D. YOUNG, *chairman of General Electric, on December 1, 1929, a month after the market crash that wiped out an estimated $30 billion in value. The market would take some twenty years to fully recover.*

I think there is a world market for maybe five computers.

> THOMAS J. WATSON SR., *chairman of IBM, in 1943.*

Video won't be able to hold on to any market it captures after the first six months. People will soon get tired of staring at a plywood box every night.

> **DARRYL F. ZANUCK**, *head of Twentieth Century Fox Studios, in 1946, on the prospects for commercial television.*

Nuclear-powered vacuum cleaners will probably be a reality in ten years.

> **ALEXANDER LEWYT**, *president of U.S. home-appliance maker Lewyt, in the mid-1950s.*

The Edsel is here to stay.

> **HENRY FORD II**, *chairman of Ford Motor, to dealers in 1957. The Edsel line was discontinued two years later.*

There is no reason why anyone would want a computer in their home.

> **KENNETH OLSEN**, *founder of computer maker Digital Equipment, dismissing the PC phenomenon in 1977.*

You can't build a software company that's bigger than ten million in sales. It's impossible. There isn't a big enough market. You can't get that many people together on a project. You can't have a software company bigger than ten million.

> **BILL GATES**, *co-founder of Microsoft, in the late 1970s. In 2001, Microsoft generated $27 billion in revenues and $6.1 billion in profits.*

The surest move ever made.

> ROBERTO GOIZUETA, *CEO of Coca-Cola, introducing the doomed New Coke in 1985.*

Bill Gates blew it with Windows. They missed their shot.

> DAVID C. COLE, *CEO of U.S. software firm Ashton-Tate and later of Ziff, in the* Wall Street Journal *in 1985, on the Microsoft operating system destined to capture 95 percent of the world market.*

Our performance has never been stronger; our business model has never been more robust; our growth has never been more certain.

> KENNETH LAY, *chairman of U.S. energy trading firm Enron, in a reassuring email message to employees in August 2001, even as he was dumping his own Enron stock prior to the firm's bankruptcy in December 2001.*

Private Companies

Being private means you don't get saddled with the professional nuts who buy one share of stock and hound you at the annual meetings.

> WILLIAM RANDOLPH HEARST JR., *chairman of Hearst Corp., publisher of* Good Housekeeping *and* Cosmopolitan, *in 1976.*

I would find it rather revolting to put up with two-share stockholders wanting to know what my profits will be in five years.

> WALTER ANNENBERG, *head of privately held Triangle Publications* (TV Guide, Seventeen, Daily Racing Form), *in 1976.*

If I knew my compensation next year would be based on this year's return on equity, hell no, I wouldn't act the same. You've only got a few years at the top in a public company to make your killing. You want to put every penny on the bottom line to wind up with the juiciest retirement package you can get.

> DAVID JONES, *president of privately held Pride Refining of Abilene, Texas, in* Fortune *in 1982.*

How many times have you made one of those tough decisions and six months later found that you were dead wrong? If you're private, you just have to explain to some of your associates or maybe your board of directors. If you're public, you're liable to keep going the wrong way so you don't look like an idiot.

> MICHAEL J. CUDAHY, *CEO of Marquette Electronics of Milwaukee, Wisconsin, a medical equipment maker, in* Fortune *in 1984.*

There's no such thing as a friendly shareholder.

> RICHARD BRANSON, *CEO of British conglomerate Virgin Group, on why he took his conglomerate private in 1990 just two years after issuing shares to the public.*

Privacy [is] morally and ethically proper and even desirable—and a key to healthy, normal living. [It] allows us to do the very best we can, the very best we know how, and to do so without being self-aggrandizing.

> **FORREST MARS JR.**, *defending his privately held confectionery and pet-food company's reputation for secrecy, cited in Joël Glenn Brenner's,* Emperors of Chocolate: Inside the Secret World of Hershey and Mars *(1999).*

If I lost control of the business, I'd lose myself—or at least the ability to be myself. Owning myself is a way to be myself.

> **OPRAH WINFREY**, *in* Fortune *in 2002, on why she refused to take her entertainment company public, in contrast to rival "living brand" Martha Stewart.*

Private Life

I'll go to jail rather than discuss my private affairs.

> **J. P. MORGAN**, *U.S. financier, in 1912 when called to testify before the congressional Pujo Committee on recent irregularities on Wall Street.*

I don't mix business with anything. I don't do business dinners. I don't do business tennis. And I don't do business squash.

> **PHILIP FREDERICK ANSCHUTZ**, *a Denver billionaire with extensive holdings in oil, hotels, entertainment, and other businesses, in 1988.*

What I'm always astounded by is that just because I have had some business success, people assume I do not have intellectual interests and intellectual capabilities.

> **MORTIMER ZUCKERMAN**, *real estate developer and sometime publisher of* Atlantic Monthly, U.S. News & World Report, *and New York's* Daily News, *in* Fortune *in 1993.*

Hegel wrote that no one is a hero to his valet, not because he isn't a hero, but because the valet is a valet.

> **CONRAD BLACK**, *later Lord Black of Crossharbour, Anglo-Canadian press baron, in a 1995 review of a biographical exposé of former Canadian prime minister Brian Mulroney in which one source is the ex-PM's household staff—"a notoriously unreliable group," Black noted, "as any experienced employer of such people knows."*

Product Development

It takes five years to develop a new car in this country. Heck, we won World War II in four years.

> **H. ROSS PEROT**, *briefly a board member at General Motors, in 1986, on the slow pace of developing new models in the U.S. auto industry.*

Sometimes I think we'll see the day when you introduce a product in the morning and announce its end of life at the end of the day.

> **ALAN F. SHUGART**, *chairman of disk-drive giant Seagate Technology, in the 1980s.*

Product development was like elephant intercourse. It was accompanied by much hooting, hollering, and throwing of dirt, and then nothing would happen for a year.

> JACK REICHERT, *CEO in the early 1990s of Illinois-based recreational products firm Brunswick, maker of billiard supplies and Mercury outboard motors.*

New technologies take time, but they are worth the wait. Did the PC catch on quickly? Come on. We were talking about them in 1975 and our first thirteen customers went bankrupt before we signed up one that survived. That was Apple.

> BILL GATES, *co-founder of Microsoft, in* Fortune *in 1990.*

Part of our appeal is we didn't change our car for fifteen years. It got to be quirky, ugly, and old, but that's what people wanted.

> KEITH O. BUTLER-WHEELHOUSE, *CEO of Swedish auto maker Saab, in 1995.*

If you're going to be cannibalized, it's best to dine with friends.

> JOHN A. ROTH, *CEO of Nortel Networks, in 1998, on making sure it's your new products, not the competition's, that make your existing line obsolete.*

Is that doo-dad actually important to people or is it just geek sex?

> STEVE BALLMER, *CEO of Microsoft, in the 1990s, with a typical query to techies proposing exotic features for new products.*

Profit

It is the straphangers that pay the dividends.

> **CHARLES TYSON YERKES**, *19th-century U.S. financier, when asked why he didn't do something about the overcrowding and long delays on his Chicago streetcar system.*

We try never to forget that medicine is for the people. It is not for the profits. The profits follow, and if we have remembered that, they have never failed to appear.

> **GEORGE MERCK II**, *CEO of U.S. drug maker Merck & Co., in 1950.*

So far as is humanly possible, we aim to get profit out of everything we do.

> **JOHN MCKEEN**, *president of Pfizer and a contemporary of George Merck II,* in Forbes *in 1962.*

Too many people think only of their own profit. But business opportunity seldom knocks on the door of self-centered people. No customer ever goes to a store merely to please the storekeeper.

> **KAZUO INAMORI**, *founder of Kyocera, a leading Japanese maker of ceramic casings for computer chips, and of DDI, Japan's second-largest phone company, cited in the* New York Times *in 1997.*

We were profitable for a brief period in December 1995. It was a mistake.

> JEFFREY P. BEZOS, *founder and CEO of Amazon.com, arguing in 1999 that profitability came second to reinvesting in his online retail enterprise.*

The bottom line is in heaven.

> EDWIN H. LAND, *father of instant photography, on the primacy of innovation over profit. The company he founded, Polaroid, was never a consistent money maker and filed for bankruptcy in 2001.*

Turnover is vanity and profits are sanity.

> FELIX DENNIS, *British magazine publisher whose firm, Dennis Publishing, published* Maxim *and other popular titles, in the London* Financial Times *in 2001.*

Public Speaking

If you're at a party, the best way to overcome shyness is by acting like a host. You forget that you're uncomfortable because you're busy making sure that everybody else is doing fine. To me, giving speeches is like hosting parties: Your role is to make everybody in the room feel comfortable.

> JIM MCCANN, *president of 1-800-Flowers, in* Forbes *in 1999.*

Many executives believe that good debating skills are the most important for learning how to make a point, but there are other ways, too. I think studying poetry gave me more of an edge. By reciting poetry you learn how to play with the words.

CAROL BARTZ, *CEO of Autodesk, in* Forbes *in 1999.*

Bill Gates asked me to go over to see him the other day. He invited thirty top chief executives from around the world and asked if I would do a ten-minute presentation. Just before I stood up to speak he handed out forms to everybody and said, "I think everybody should mark Richard one to ten for his presentation." I thought fuck, I want to get straight on the plane and go home. This is the strangest thing I've ever come across.

SIR RICHARD BRANSON, *CEO of British conglomerate Virgin Group, in London's* Sunday Telegraph *in 2001.*

I couldn't deliver a speech to save my life. Before reading my first speech in front of a few hundred GE executives in Cooperstown, N.Y., I twice had to leave the front row of the auditorium to run to the bathroom.

JACK WELCH, *CEO of General Electric, in his 2001 memoir,* Jack: Straight from the Gut, *on one of the handicaps he had to overcome in climbing the executive ladder at GE.*

Quality

I have always believed that quality is remembered long after the price is forgotten.

> STANLEY MARCUS, *president of Texas carriage-trade retailer Neiman Marcus.*

Nothing that costs only a dollar is worth having.

> ELIZABETH ARDEN, *U.S. cosmetics entrepreneur, a rival to Revlon and Estée Lauder in the 1950s.*

The slogan constantly put pressure on us to make Hallmark cards "the very best." We have thrown away millions of cards that did not justify that commitment. I somehow feel that without the slogan our products would not have been as good.

> JOYCE C. HALL, *founder of Hallmark Cards of Kansas City, Missouri, the leading U.S. maker of greeting cards, in his 1979 memoir,* When You Care Enough. *The company adopted the motto, "When you care enough to send the very best," in 1944.*

I truly believe that one of the things we missed as an industry is the quality issue. For $250 you can buy a CD player that produces better sound than any computer except Next. Why should a $300 VCR outperform a several-thousand-dollar computer? There is something wrong with that.

> STEVE JOBS, *co-founder of Apple Computer, in* Forbes *in 1991.*

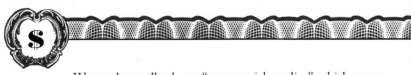

We used to talk about "commercial quality," which meant that you expected to have a certain amount of defects.

> ROBERT STEMPEL, *president of General Motors, in* Time *in 1989.*

Absolute maximum growth is probably incompatible with maximum quality.

> LARRY ELLISON, *founder and CEO of California-based computer software giant Oracle, in* Forbes *in 1990.*

The ancient Romans had a tradition. Whenever one of their engineers constructed an arch, as the capstone was hoisted into place, the engineer assumed accountability for his work in the most profound way possible: he stood under the arch.

> C. MICHAEL ARMSTRONG, *CEO of Hughes Electronics and later of AT&T, in a 1995 speech.*

Real Estate

It is gratifying to build a monument.

> PAUL REICHMANN, *chief strategist of the family-owned Olympia & York Developments, developer of New York's World Financial Center and London's Canary Wharf, which plunged O&Y into bankruptcy in 1992, in* Maclean's *in 1981. Reichmann was referring to an early O&Y triumph, Toronto's First Canadian Place, head office of the Bank of Montreal and the tallest bank headquarters building in the world when it was completed in the mid-1970s.*

Could I begin life again, knowing what I now know, and had money to invest, I would buy every foot of land on the Island of Manhattan.

> JOHN JACOB ASTOR, *a fur trader turned land developer, who was one of the largest landlords in Manhattan by the 1820s.*

The tarantula and real estate agent alike live off the tenderfoot.

> WILLIAM RANDOLPH HEARST, *U.S. newspaper mogul, in 1915.*

Stay out in the country. That's the new downtown.

> EDWARD JOHN DEBARTOLO, *Ohio-based pioneer developer of suburban shopping centers, launching his firm in 1948.*

Look at every Main Street of every town in America and ask yourself "who cares?" Nobody cares about community, divinity, and humanity, and you can prove it by asking people what they do care about. In terms of shelter they care about downpayment and location. Give me downpayment and location and I'll outsell community, divinity, and humanity on any street corner.

> VICTOR H. PALMIERI, *U.S. land developer, later a corporate turnaround artist, in Kaiser News in 1966.*

Don't sell. Tough it out, tough it out, tough it out.

> TRAMMELL CROW, *Dallas developer who narrowly averted disaster in a 1974 real estate crunch, and whose firm was humbled again in the early 1990s meltdown in North American real estate values, in the 1990s.*

I like to buy land, since it brings you money in your sleep.

> **SEIJURO MATSUOKA**, *a Japanese land developer whose real estate interests were valued at about $2 billion in 1987.*

Times Square is like the Bermuda Triangle—investments made there are never heard from again.

> **SEYMOUR B. DURST**, *New York real estate developer, in* Forbes *in 1988.*

For the Japanese, land is gold. So if you see land, think of it as a lump of gold spread over the ground.

> **HARUHIKO YOSHIMOTO**, *Osaka developer who held about $3.1 billion worth of Osaka land in 1990.*

The goddam real estate business. It's the graveyard of the human ego.

> **PETER MUNK**, *Canadian real estate mogul, whose company TrizecHahn dumped assets in a late 1990s market reversal after acquiring such landmark properties as Chicago's Sears Tower, the Watergate office-apartment complex in Washington, D.C., and Toronto's CN Tower.*

Religion

God gave me my money.

> **JOHN D. ROCKEFELLER SR.**, *U.S. oil monopolist founder, in the late 19th century.*

He picked up twelve men from the bottom rank of business and forged them into an organization that conquered the world.

> BRUCE BARTON, *co-founder of U.S. advertising agency BBDO, in his 1920 book about Jesus,* The Man Nobody Knows. *"Christ," said Barton, "would be a national advertiser today, I am sure, as He was a great advertiser in His own day. He thought of His life as business."*

I pray for Milky Way. I pray for Snickers.

> FORREST MARS SR., *who, on taking complete ownership of his father's candy company in 1964, gathered executives in a conference room at the firm's Chicago plant. "I'm a religious man," he said, then got down on his knees and began to pray for each Mars brand.*

REALITY CHECK

The rich man is the moral man. Godliness is in league with riches.

> WILLIAM LAURENCE, *Episcopal bishop, preaching in the late 19th century to a New York congregation that included in its number the financier J. P. Morgan.*

Just in terms of allocation of time resources, religion is not very efficient. There's a lot more I could be doing on a Sunday morning.

> BILL GATES, *co-founder of Microsoft, in* Time *in 1999.*

I think God is using this company as a vehicle. I'm trying to take the beautiful creatures He created and help them reach down within themselves to bring out all the ability He gave them.

MARY KAY ASH, *founder of Dallas-based Mary Kay Cosmetics, in the early 1980s.*

It's true that there's plenty of evil in the world, but the level of faithfulness is greater in the business world than in other fields.

SIR JOHN TEMPLETON, *mutual fund manager, in Fortune in 1989. Templeton, who began business meetings with a nonsectarian prayer, said an investor who asks for God's guidance is "less likely to make stupid mistakes."*

Research and Development

Let your light so shine—that those who seek the Truth, that those who toil that this world may be a better place to live in, that those who hold aloft that torch of Science and Knowledge through these social and economic dark ages, shall take new courage and feel their hands supported.

GEORGE W. MERCK, *CEO of U.S. drug maker Merck & Co., at the 1933 opening of the Merck Research Laboratory.*

I have learned to have more faith in the scientist than he does in himself.

> **DAVID SARNOFF**, *founder of RCA, who introduced commercial television at the 1939 World's Fair in New York.*

We will not do less research and development work. We will not discharge the people we have trained. We will all work for nothing if we have to.

> **WILLIS H. CARRIER**, *air-conditioning pioneer, dictating the terms by which his struggling firm would accept a rescue plan proposed by Chicago banker Cloud Wampler, who later became CEO of the Carrier Corp., cited in Margaret Ingels's,* Father of Air Conditioning *(1952).*

Mahoney's First Rule of R&D—if you cite an R&D project in the chairman's letter in the annual report, the project will enjoy perpetual funding whether or not it even sees the light of day in the marketplace.

Mahoney's Second Rule of R&D is that you must keep reminding your research staff in companies like Monsanto that you're in business to sell products. We are all gratified by advancing the frontiers of scientific knowledge, but the only thing that ever gets invoiced is the product.

> **RICHARD J. MAHONEY**, *CEO of St. Louis-based chemical firm Monsanto, in a 1993 speech.*

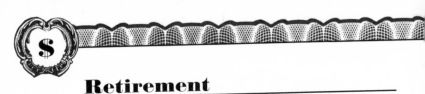

Retirement

My work is done. Why wait?

> **GEORGE EASTMAN**, *founder of Eastman Kodak, suicide note in 1932.*

I never thought I'd make it big. If I felt I had made it, I would be somewhere nice, like St. Moritz, skiing.

> **ESTÉE LAUDER**, *née Josephine Esther Mentzer, 20th-century cosmetics entrepreneur, still active in managing Estée Lauder Inc. into her seventies, by which point the firm had overtaken longtime archrival Revlon.*

There's no rainbow out there with "Retirement" written across it. If you're not enjoying the ride, get off the train.

> **GEORGE MOORE**, *longtime CEO of First National City Bank, forerunner of Citibank, who spearheaded the bank's global expansion in the mid-20th century, telling young executives that a career is supposed to be about making friends and having fun, not dying rich.*

I am too old. I have no willingness to learn new technology anymore.

> **SOICHIRO HONDA**, *announcing his retirement in 1973 at age sixty-seven from the Japanese automaker he had founded.*

I wish I could wake up stone-broke to see if I could create lots of wealth again.

> **H. L. HUNT**, *Texas oilman, a few years before his death in 1974, when he left a personal fortune of $2 billion to his five sons and five daughters from two marriages.*

Retirement for me means kill me.

TONY ROSSI, *CEO of U.S. juice company Tropicana, in* Fortune *in 1978, on why he resisted a takeover by cereal maker Kellogg Co. that would have put him out of a job.*

REALITY CHECK

The idol of today pushes the hero of yesterday out of our recollection; and will, in turn, be supplanted by his successor of tomorrow.

WASHINGTON IRVING

People who are at all observant see how quickly the prestige mantle falls away when you retire. The prestige of the job is not something one wants to bank one's feelings on very much.

CHARLES L. BROWN, *CEO of AT&T, in 1980.*

When top management reaches sixty-five, they ought to get out. They know a lot of things that aren't true anymore.

WALTER WRISTON, *who retired as CEO of Citicorp in 1984.*

Everyone should have an Italian afterlife.

EDWIN ARTZT, *departing CEO of Cincinnati-based Procter & Gamble, reveling in his imminent move to Italy as executive director at G&R Barilla, Italy's largest pasta maker.*

You stop being on the A list, your calls don't get returned. It's not just less fawning—people couldn't care less about you in some cases. The king is dead. Long live the king.

> **DAVID MAHONEY**, *former CEO of U.S. conglomerate Norton Simon, in the* New York Times *in 1993.*

It's painful. Even though you knew it was a game, you learn the hard way that you had your turn, and now a new guy gets his.

> **IRVING SHAPIRO**, *CEO of DuPont from 1974 to 1981, reflecting on retirement in a 1996 interview in* Fortune.

Well, I really don't know because I don't believe in doctors. But number one, I feel fine. Number two, I swim a mile every day. And number three, I'm single, so I get laid all the time.

> **PETER BENJAMIN LEWIS**, *CEO of U.S. financial services conglomerate Progressive, asked about his health by a prospective investor who wondered about his proximity to retirement.*

I had this wonderful romantic Bohemian image of me with a ponytail, banging out bad books, and meeting nice people and being barefoot and all that stuff. It lasted about four nanoseconds and I ended up at Barclays.

> **MATTHEW W. BARRETT**, *CEO of Barclays, the largest bank in Britain, in a London* Sunday Telegraph *interview in 2002. Before taking the helm at Barclays in 1999, Barrett was contemplating retirement after almost a decade as CEO of Canada's Bank of Montreal.*

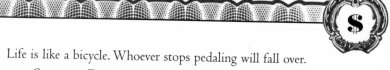

Life is like a bicycle. Whoever stops pedaling will fall over.

> SABASTIAO FERRAZ DE CAMRGO PENTEADO, *on his determination to remain active as head of the biggest construction company in Brazil.*

Ripostes

No. And at the directors' meeting this morning, we voted that you could ask that question of only one director.

> DONALD GRAHAM, *CEO of the* Washington Post, *responding to a question from a shareholder at an annual meeting in the 1980s on whether Graham had ever committed adultery.*

I went up to him with a big smile and said I appreciated the compliments. In the office I'm known as a fascist.

> JOHN BOGLE SR., *founder of U.S. index mutual fund pioneer Vanguard Funds, after being attacked as a communist and Marxist by a speaker at a funds conference.*

Maybe you will, Henry. Maybe you will. And when I want a monkey, Henry, I'll send for you.

> JAY GOULD, *19th-century U.S. railroad speculator, after he was confronted by Henry Smith, a rival whom he had bested. Smith had sputtered, "I will live to see the day, sir, when you have to earn a living by going around this street with a hand organ and a monkey."*

He curtly informed me of his intention to buy my business so that he could be the Cadillac of the cosmetics industry. I replied lightly that I thought his intention quite flattering, but that I would like to buy his business and be the Rolls-Royce of the industry. Not known for his sense of humor, he stalked away without answering. War was declared. "I'll destroy her," he told some mutual friends.

> **ESTÉE LAUDER**, *20th-century U.S. cosmetics entrepreneur, recalling in her memoir a rare encounter with archrival Charles Revson.*

Well, bull. I run what this year will be a $300 million company in sales. I'm older than John Kennedy was when he got elected President. And we've had eight good years back to back.

> **T. J. RODGERS**, *CEO of Cypress Semiconductor of San Jose, California, in 1991. Some rivals were saying that the maverick Rodgers, then forty-three, who had earned his PhD at Stanford University, was a kid who needed to grow up.*

I personally evaluate the future of MMM as glittering. Even the danger of the accidental arrest of our leadership no longer threatens us. I am already in prison, and they can't do more than that.

> **SERGEI MAVRODI**, *president of MMM, a Russian mutual fund accused of defrauding millions of investors in a pyramid scheme, in a 1994 open letter published in Russian newspapers.*

Role Models

Max Ward changed the standard for charter flights and the public image of them. And, by setting new higher standards, he eventually forced airlines many times the size of Wardair to upgrade.

> **ISADORE SHARP**, *founder of Four Seasons Hotels, in 1980. Wardair, the low-cost airline noted for gourmet meals served on real china, was rated the world's best charter carrier in the mid-1980s, before folding later in the decade because of overexpansion when it was absorbed by a larger rival.*

I have six of your TVs in my house.

> **PHIL KNIGHT**, *co-founder of Nike, introducing himself to Sony co-founder Akio Morita, whom he had sought out in Japan for marketing advice. "I have a pair of your sneakers in my closet," said Morita.*

How can an ugly little guy who isn't even really French manage to rise up and rewrite the laws of Europe so that even today the Code Napoleon is a big thing? And the way he recognized scientific and artistic leaders of the time…. This is one smart guy.

> **BILL GATES**, *co-founder of Microsoft, on Napoleon, whose life had been an inspiration to Gates since adolescence. Cited in Stephen Manes and Paul Andrews's,* Gates: How Microsoft's Mogul Reinvented an Industry and Made Himself the Richest Man in America *(1993).*

3M! No doubt about it. You never know what they're going to come up with next. The beauty of it is that they probably don't know what they're going to come up with next either. But even though you can never predict what exactly the company will do, you know that it will continue to be successful.

WILLIAM (BILL) HEWLETT, *co-founder of Hewlett-Packard, asked to name the firm he most admired, in James C. Collins and Jerry I. Porras's,* Built to Last: Successful Habits of Visionary Companies *(1994).*

In choosing my father, my mother deliberately chose a man who would see her as an equal. When she spoke, he listened. She handled the family's finances, and I never heard him question how she spent a dollar. Seeing how influential she was helped me immeasurably in developing my own independence. Probably because of that gender-neutral household, I have expected to be defined by—and succeed because of—values, character and intellect.

ANNE M. MULCAHY, *CEO of Xerox, in the* New York Times *in 2001.*

Selling

Touch your customer and you're halfway there.

ESTÉE LAUDER, *20th-century U.S. cosmetics magnate, counseling sales clerks to offer free demonstrations of the product.*

Avoid all extravagant expressions in selling. If the value is good your customer will not have difficulty in discovering it.

> **TIMOTHY EATON**, *founder of Canadian department store chain T. Eaton Co., in an 1894 speech to his top managers.*

No man is too big to go out and make a sale.

> **STANLEY MARCUS**, *president of Dallas carriage-trade retailer Neiman Marcus, who personally sold more than $10 million worth of furs, including a $125,000 mink coat that Richard Burton bought for then-wife Elizabeth Taylor in the 1960s.*

Pretend that every single person you meet has a sign around his or her neck that says, "Make me feel important."

> **MARY KAY ASH**, *cosmetics entrepreneur who founded Dallas-based Mary Kay Cosmetics in 1963, advising her sales associates on a key aspect of selling.*

The difference between rape and rapture is salesmanship.

> **ROY THOMSON**, *Anglo-Canadian press baron, who by the mid-1960s had built an international media empire.*

You have to remember who pays the bills. No matter what the primary discipline—finance, manufacturing—you have to know and experience the excitement of sales. That's where you really see things happen.

> **JOHN OPEL**, *CEO of IBM.*

If someone doesn't want your product, never answer with "Yes, but…" With the first "Yes, but," argument creeps in, and this serves no good purpose in selling. It takes two people to make an argument, and the salesman should never be one of them.

    THOMAS J. WATSON SR., *founder of IBM, which he joined in 1914 when it was the Computing-Tabulating-Recording Co., advising his salespeople to win over prospects by appearing to agree with them.*

We have an expression around here: When you're out there selling, make sure you take care of the business that you've got, so the rug doesn't get rolled up behind you.

    CURT CARLSON, *founder of Minneapolis-based hospitality conglomerate Carlson Cos. in* Forbes *in 1989.*

A salesman should be able to sell horse apples. You just have to con the sonofabitch.

    LEONARD STERN, *owner of U.S. pet supplies firm Hartz Mountain Industries and sometime publisher of the* Village Voice.

Size

A great business is really too big to be human. It grows so large as to supplant the personality of the man. The modern worker finds himself part of an organization which leaves him little initiative.

    HENRY FORD, *founder in 1903 of Ford Motor.*

We got bloody big, and it's difficult for a big agency to be good. But I wouldn't be living at my château had we remained small.

> **DAVID MACKENZIE OGILVY**, *co-founder of advertising agency Ogilvy & Mather, in* Business Week *in 1986. In the mid-1970s, Ogilvy quit Manhattan for France, continuing to work for his agency from the baronial splendor of his Château de Touffou.*

You can build a computer in a garage. You can have a great idea for a drug. But to get the ultimate molecule takes enormous effort, and it's not going to be done in a garage.

> **DR. P. ROY VAGELOS**, *CEO of Merck & Co., in* Fortune *in 1987.*

Management always likes bigger companies. To get smaller seemed wimpish. But I knew from the start that it would release new energies.

> **SIR CHRISTOPHER HOGG**, *head of British textile firm Courtaulds and later chairman of Reuters Group, Allied Domecq, and GlaxoSmithKline, on why he split up the venerable Courtaulds in 1990 into two leaner companies.*

Chevrolet is such a big monster that you twist its tail and nothing happens at the other end for months and months. It is so gigantic that there isn't any way to really run it. You just sort of keep track of it.

> **ELLIOT M. ESTES**, *president of Chevrolet parent General Motors, cited by Michigan State University professor Walter Adams in a 1991 report.*

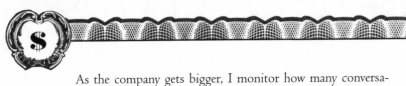

As the company gets bigger, I monitor how many conversations I have to have with people inside Nortel before I can say yes to a customer. When you're having too many of these conversations you know you're no longer agile.

> **JOHN A. ROTH**, *CEO of Nortel Networks, based in Brampton, Ontario, in 2001.*

Scale matters, and bigger seems to mean better to most managers. Maybe it's critical mass, or technology and globalization, or integration, or sheer vanity and ego, but there is a natural imperative toward scale.

> **BRUCE WASSERSTEIN**, *top U.S. merger and acquisitions dealmaker, in 2001.*

We are certainly more visible today. As a big company, one has the handicap of deep pockets.

> **THIERRY DESMAREST**, *CEO of French oil giant TotalFinaElf, which was increasingly targeted by environmental and human rights groups as it grew in size, in London's* Financial Times *in 2002.*

Spouses

Why can't we end all of this nonsense? You can puree tomatoes at the plant, why not vegetables for Sally?

> **DOROTHY GERBER** *to her husband, Daniel F. Gerber, who was inspired to retrofit his father's canning plant to make baby food, in 1927.*

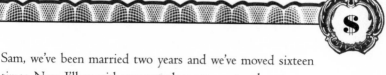

Sam, we've been married two years and we've moved sixteen times. Now, I'll go with you any place you want so long as you don't ask me to live in a big city. Ten thousand people is enough for me.

> HELEN R. WALTON, *wife of peripatetic merchant Sam Walton, holding out for Bentonville, Arkansas, as the home base for the new Wal-Mart chain her husband launched in 1962. By 2001, when it was the largest company in the world, with $218 billion in annual sales, Wal-Mart was still represented mostly in the towns and small cities of the U.S. heartland.*

If women didn't exist, all the money in the world would have no meaning.

> ARISTOTLE ONASSIS, *who in 1968 gave his new wife, Jacqueline Kennedy, $3 million up front, $5 million worth of jewelry in their first year of marriage, and a $30,000 monthly allowance.*

Dear, never forget one little point. It's my business. You just work here.

> ELIZABETH ARDEN, *cosmetics entrepreneur, to her husband, in Alfred A. Lewis and Constance Woodworth's,* Miss Elizabeth Arden *(1972).*

Each of them was jealous and resentful of my preoccupation with business. Yet none showed any visible aversion to sharing in the proceeds.

> J. PAUL GETTY, *U.S. oilman, on his wives, in his 1976 memoir,* As I See It.

Miuccia was such a first-rate worker and designer, I knew it would be cheaper in the long run to marry her.

PATRIZIO BERTELLI, *CEO of Italian fashion house Prada, who in 1978 met Miuccia Prada, third-generation heiress of a luxury luggage maker founded in 1913.*

REALITY CHECK

When you married me you wanted Lancelot. And now you'll settle for George Babbitt. I suppose that's the story of the American wife.

LOUIS AUCHINLOSS, *Honorable Men (1985)*

My newly developed standard response is, the less I say about it, the better; and the more I *do* about it, the better.

MORTIMER ZUCKERMAN, *U.S. media and real estate baron, in 1992 on his own puzzlement at having remained single.*

Get a mate who will allow you to work day and night seven days a week, if need be. Otherwise stay single.

LUIGINO FRANCESCO PAULUCCI, *U.S. land developer and founder of food-processing companies Chun King and Jeno's frozen pizza, who had an estimated net worth of $350 million in 1984.*

[The wife] is much more important in business today than most people realize. The right wife can be a big help. There's a great deal of after-hours socializing in these executive groups, and the right wife gets friendly with the other right wives and helps her husband along. But he may not be the best man for the job at all, so the wife's work may be bad for the company although good for her husband.

> LAURENCE TISCH, *U.S. merchant banker, in John Train's,* The Money Masters *(1979).*

See that your daughters marry outstanding men.

> CHARLES MURPHY JR., *20th-century U.S. oilman, founder of Murphy Oil of El Dorado, Arkansas, on the secret to his family firm's success.*

I have discovered that you can do business without living with business people. I was never going to be the wife of someone like that.

> BARONESS PHILIPPINE DE ROTHSCHILD, *who appeared for many years on stage at the Comédie Française, where she met actor and later estranged husband Phillippine Pascal, before inheriting her father's winery empire in 1987. By 2002, she had built up the holdings to include the renowned Château Mouton Rothschild Bordeaux, Château d'Armailhac, and Château Clerc Milon estate wineries in France, plus a joint venture with California wine-maker Robert Mondavi. Cited in* EuroBusiness *in 2002.*

Strategic Planning

If we ever have a plan, we're screwed.

> PAUL NEWMAN, *U.S. actor and salad-dressing entrepreneur, in the 1980s.*

People ask me what my three-year plan is. I say, "What about a three-month plan?"

> LARRY ELLISON, *who co-founded U.S. computer software firm Oracle in 1977 with $1,200 in start-up capital, in the 1990s.*

Our three hundred-year plan is the long-term structure we need to fit our goals. Long horizons change your priorities.

> MASAYOSHI-SON, *founder of Internet empire Softbank of Japan, an early investor in Yahoo! and 130 other firms, in the 1990s.*

Columbus didn't have a business plan when he discovered America.

> ANDREW S. GROVE, *CEO of Intel, in the* New Yorker *in 1994. Grove was making the point that to "make money, companies must be prepared to lose money."*

We try a bunch of stuff, we see what works, and we call that our strategy.

> DENNIS BAKKE, *CEO of U.S. electric power distribution firm AES, in 1999.*

For seventeen years Body Shop never had a marketing department, no business plan, no job descriptions. We knew the first names of everyone's grandmother, but we were falling apart at the seams. You'd bury your head with laughter if you saw how unprofessional we are.

> ANITA RODDICK, *founder of Body Shop International, a retailer of all-natural cosmetics, in 1996, twenty years after she and her husband launched the firm, which they initially ran from their home in southern England.*

REALITY CHECK

However beautiful the strategy, you should occasionally look at the results.

WINSTON CHURCHILL

Getting the right people in the right jobs is a lot more important than developing a strategy. We learned the hard way that we could have the greatest strategies in the world. Without the right leaders developing and owning them, we'd get good-looking presentations and so-so results.

> JACK WELCH, *CEO of General Electric, in his 2001 memoir,* Jack: Straight from the Gut. *Welch noted that GE's leadership in medical equipment can be traced to putting a zealot in charge of the area, in which GE had previously floundered for a decade.*

If I called a strategic planning meeting, there would be dead silence, and then people would fall out of their chairs laughing.

> **OPRAH WINFREY**, *90 percent owner of Chicago-based Harpo, a $988 million entertainment conglomerate, in* Fortune *in 2002.*

Success

The crowd is all ready to help tear down a successful—the most successful singer, or speaker, or lawmaker, the most successful in any endeavor. Who were we that we should succeed where so many others failed? Of course, there was something wrong, some dark, evil mystery, or we never should have succeeded.

> **JOHN D. ROCKEFELLER SR.**, *on muckrakers who attacked his Standard Oil trust, in the late 19th century.*

Formula for success: Rise early, work hard, strike oil.

> **J. PAUL GETTY**, *20th-century U.S. oilman.*

If you think very long about the things you did right, you'll be in serious trouble.

> **KEN OLSEN**, *founder in 1957 of U.S. computer maker Digital Equipment.*

So many people have claimed to be the father of the Mustang that I wouldn't want to be seen in public with the mother.

> LEE IACOCCA, *president of Ford Motor, who spearheaded Ford's most successful new-product launch of the 1960s.*

Appetite, luck, the right people, and fear.

> SIR JAMES GOLDSMITH, *British financier, prominent as a hostile takeover artist in the 1980s, on attributes for success.*

We've already had a million Germans and a million British guests, and to have those numbers in France without a war going on is really something.

> MICHAEL D. EISNER, *CEO of Walt Disney Co., on the success of the EuroDisney theme park near Paris, in the 1990s.*

Business success contains the seeds of its own destruction.... When the curve shifts and a different set of skills are needed, the past selection process has gotten you a management that is not in tune with the new one.

> ANDREW S. GROVE, *CEO of Intel, in* Report on Business Magazine *in 1996.*

Success is a lousy teacher. It seduces smart people into thinking they can't lose.

> BILL GATES, *co-founder of Microsoft.*

Succession

I often live off the carnage of failed management development programs. The president of the company should help to develop his executive vice-presidents, and he should be measured according to the successors he has developed. Lots of people don't do that. It's why I make my money.

> GERALD ROCHE, *chairman of U.S. executive recruitment firm Heidrick & Struggles, in* Forbes *in 1983.*

Nobody told me before I became president.

> FRED L. HARTLEY, *CEO of California oil company Unocal, when asked if he would name his successor, in the* Wall Street Journal *in 1985.*

I'm totally healthy. I'm fifty-two years old. What I need is help, not succession.

> MICHAEL D. EISNER, *CEO of Walt Disney, after his coronary bypass, in* Business Week *in 1994.*

If you've been chairman and running things, you shouldn't sit there and second guess your successor. If you're going to get out, get out.

> RICHARD JENRETTE, *retired chairman of Equitable Cos. and investment bank Donaldson Lufkin & Jenrette, in the* Wall Street Journal *in 1996.*

If you're twenty-one, it's nice to know the boss has to get out and make room for others. If you look at the companies where the CEO stayed till he's eighty, those are the people who confuse themselves with their company. That's a fatal mistake.

> WALTER WRISTON, *former CEO of Citicorp, in the* New York Times *in 1993.*

Some chief executives just have carpet under their fingernails—you have to drag 'em out of the office.

> F. ROSS JOHNSON, *former CEO of RJR Nabisco, in the 1990s. Johnson had the opposite problem: Only a few years after taking over RJR Nabisco, he was anxious to cash out of the firm in a disastrous, $25 billion leveraged buyout of the company in 1989.*

The dynamic of having the old CEO hang around in order to be helpful to the new CEO is almost always nonsense. It can create two problems. The successor may not want to make changes because he doesn't want to hurt the feelings of his predecessor. And the person who is being succeeded may feel resentment if something is changed. The old CEO ought to go away, and if the new CEO has a question, he can call him or have lunch with him.

> HARVEY GOLUB, *CEO of American Express, in a 2000* Business Week *interview. When he was replaced as CEO in 2001 by his chosen successor, Kenneth I. Chenault, Golub quit the Amex board.*

I wanted to pick someone young enough to be in the job for at least a decade. While a CEO can have an immediate impact, I always felt people should live with their decisions and especially with their mistakes. I certainly had. Someone with less time might be tempted to make some crazy moves to put his stamp on the company. I've seen too many examples of that. Some companies have run through five or six different CEOs during my years as chairman. I didn't want that to happen at GE.

> JACK WELCH, *CEO of General Electric for twenty years, on the appointment of his hand-picked successor, Jeffrey Immelt, in his 2001 memoir,* Jack: Straight from the Gut.

The most important thing that Jack can do now, so I can really take the reins, is to leave. I could always call him and ask him for advice. But, physically, the business can only have one leader.

> JEFFREY IMMELT, *incoming CEO of General Electric, in July 2001, on outgoing CEO Jack Welch. At a managers' meeting seven months earlier, Immelt talked about his predecessor's long shadow, saying "everybody at GE thinks they work for Jack; every customer thinks they buy from Jack; every political person thinks they deal with Jack."*

Taxes

Why shouldn't the American people take half my money from me? I took all of it from them.

> EDWARD A. FILENE, *U.S. department store magnate, cited in Arthur Schlesinger Jr.'s,* The Coming of the New Deal *(1959).*

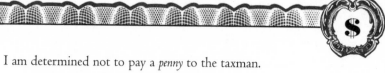

I am determined not to pay a *penny* to the taxman.

> **SIR RICHARD BRANSON,** *founder of British conglomerate Virgin Group, in 1979, when his methods for evading Her Majesty's Inland Revenue included claiming as expenses the upkeep on his plush London townhouse, his Oxfordshire country estate, and his private island, which doubled as recording studios and havens for musicians on his Virgin label.*

Some of them are afraid of terrorists—you know, the IRS.

> **MALCOLM FORBES,** *U.S. magazine publisher, explaining why some tycoons seek to avoid mention in the annual* Forbes 400 *list of America's wealthiest people, in the 1980s.*

Only the little people pay taxes.

> **LEONA HELMSLEY,** *New York hotel owner, convicted of tax evasion in the 1990s. She inherited the real estate empire of husband Harry Helmsley on his death in 1997, and in 2001 had an estimated net worth of $1.8 billion.*

Writing checks to the IRS that include strings of zeroes does not bother Charlie or me. Berkshire as a corporation, and we as individuals, have prospered in America as we would have in no other country. Indeed, if we lived in some other part of the world and completely escaped taxes, I'm sure we would be worse off financially, and in many other ways as well.

> **WARREN BUFFETT,** *CEO of Berkshire Hathaway, in his 1998 letter to shareholders. In 1998, Buffett and Berkshire vice-chairman Charlie Munger signed checks for $2.7 billion in federal taxes, equal to about half a day's federal government expenditures.*

For anyone who lives in Germany and pays taxes, ten million is a very high sum.

> **FRIEDRICH KARL FLICK**, *billionaire German industrialist who initially balked at paying the DM10 million ($6.25 million) ransom to kidnappers who grabbed his brother-in-law.*

Tough Bosses

Every successful enterprise requires three men—a dreamer, a businessman, and a son-of-a-bitch.

> **PETER MCARTHUR**, *late-19th-century British newspaper publisher.*

Really big people are, above everything else, courteous, considerate and generous—not just to some people in some circumstances, but to everyone all the time.

> **THOMAS J. WATSON SR.**, *founder of the modern IBM, which he had headed since the early 20th century, Watson Sr. was notoriously sharp-tongued with subordinates who did not bend to his will, including his own son and heir apparent, Thomas J. Watson Jr.*

There are no geniuses who work from nine to five. If anyone here doesn't like the business, he had better get out because it's too demanding.

> **EDWARD N. NEY**, *CEO of U.S. advertising firm Young & Rubicam International, in 1973. On becoming CEO of the then ailing firm in 1970, Ney cut head-office staff by 25 percent, and remaining staff were thereafter bound to be at their desks at 7:30 AM as well as 7:30 PM.*

When the bad guys start shooting you get under the table, and when they kill each other off, you surface and go to work.

> LEO JAFFE, *chairman emeritus of Columbia Pictures, in 1981, on how he survived fifty-one years' worth of office politics at the studio.*

I love to step on toes. That's my M.O.

> LAWRENCE RAWL, *CEO of Exxon, in* Fortune *in 1987.*

Okay, whose cock's on the anvil this time?

> F. ROSS JOHNSON, *CEO of RJR Nabisco in the late 1980s, when he enjoyed reminding project leaders in meetings of the stakes if they failed.*

REALITY CHECK

They sit about in groups...as if passing the pipe of peace; though, in fact, most of them are smoking cigars and some of them are eating cigars.... I fancy that all those hard-featured faces, in spectacles and shaven jaws, do look rather alike because they all like to make their faces hard.

> **G. K. CHESTERTON,** *on his visit to the United States in 1922.*

I've never thrown a telephone at anyone in my life.

> BARRY DILLER, *U.S. entertainment mogul, in the early 1990s, on his reputation for being short-tempered.*

Now that I was on top, I knew others would want to topple me.... I believe in practicing the S.O.B.'s Golden Rule: *Expect others to do unto you what you would do to them.*

> **AL NEUHARTH**, *former CEO of U.S. newspaper chain Gannett, in his 1989 memoir,* Confessions of an S.O.B.

I was a demanding and tough manager. I was no joy to behold. You have to kick some people around and remove people. You don't hesitate. You do it.

> **T. A. (THORNTON) WILSON**, *CEO of Boeing from 1969 to 1986, in* Fortune *in 1989.*

I wanted all the executives of IBM to feel the urgency I felt; whatever they did, it was never enough.

> **THOMAS J. WATSON JR.**, *CEO of IBM, in his 1990 memoir,* Father, Son & Co. *Watson even reassigned his own brother, Dick, whose spearheading of IBM's drive into mainframe computers faltered in the early going.*

You're eunuchs. How can your wives stand you? You've got nothing between your legs.

> **LINDA WACHNER**, *CEO of intimate-apparel maker Warnaco, to a group of male executives, cited in* Fortune *in 1993.*

Strive for respect. If you want somebody to like you, get a dog. I've got two; I hedged.

> **ALBERT (CHAINSAW AL) DUNLAP**, *CEO of Scott Paper and Sunbeam, in 1995.*

I am prepared to watch you lose your house and your family, for real.

> **T. J. RODGERS**, *co-founder and CEO of Cypress Semiconductor, based in San Jose, California, to a vice-president whose paycheck wasn't issued because he had fallen behind in his employee evaluations and who confronted Rodgers about his missing pay. Rodgers, who candidly described life at Cypress as "crawling through a muddy battlefield," liked to put on what he described as his "drooling psycho face" when discussing problems with his subordinates, featuring bulging veins and narrowed eyes, accompanied by fist pounding and verbal lashings.*

I used to practice what I jokingly referred to as "management by ridicule." People would be terrified to come into meetings.

> **LARRY ELLISON**, *co-founder and CEO of U.S. software giant Oracle, interviewed in Mark Leibovich's, The New Imperialists (2002).*

I sobbed real tears and I ripped off my gold watch and threw it at them because there was no more time.... "You let me down, how could you let me down, I cannot bear this, my God, I don't know what to do!" I was magnificent.

> **MARY WELLS LAWRENCE**, *former CEO of New York advertising agency Wells Rich Greene, recalling in 2002 her calculated theatrics in remonstrating subordinates for producing shoddy roughs for a proposed Pan Am ad campaign in the 1970s.*

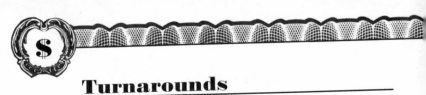

Turnarounds

The years at CertainTeed were terrific. At some companies you can work yourself to death and not find in the fifth decimal place of their earnings what you did. In my case there was very dramatic, seismic proof.

> **DONALD E. MEADS,** *who turned around CertainTeed, a Pennsylvania-based building materials firm, while CEO from 1974 to 1978.*

Big companies don't value risk-taking. There's no way I would have been chosen if they hadn't been in deep shit.

> **JOHN HARVEY-JONES,** *appointed CEO of the troubled Imperial Chemical Industries (ICI) in 1982. He revived the firm, a model of industrial leadership in the Thatcher era, and was later portrayed as a hero in the TV series* Troubleshooter.

That doesn't mean we have any magic answers or that we're going to pull a rabbit out of the hat. In fact, we have to put one in the hat before we can pull it out.

> **VICTOR H. PALMIERI,** *newly appointed CEO of troubled U.S. financial conglomerate Baldwin United, in 1983. The company was beyond salvation and survived only in its original form, as a maker of musical instruments.*

I have achieved the objectives. At times, I had thought they were dreams. Ferrari has left its mark on the last year of the old millennium and the first of the new one. It has won against BMW, Mercedes, Renault, Ford, against the world's great powers. Now I ask myself: but is it really worth it? It is a job that involves you totally and life goes by so quickly. I thank my colleagues. But my family has paid a high price.

> LUCA DI MONTEZEMOLO, *CEO of Ferrari, who turned around the legendary Italian sports-car maker and its Formula One team after the firm began to falter with the 1991 death of CEO Enzo Ferrari.*

In my experience it's very political.... You literally are reaching out and persuading everybody of everything. If you weren't, you couldn't in a relatively short time like ninety days persuade a bunch of people who didn't want to sell businesses to sell them, persuade a bunch of people who didn't want to cut a quarter of a billion dollars out of the capital budget to do it, persuade a bunch of people who felt they were earning as much as their businesses could produce to double their net operating income in the subsequent year.

> MICHAEL H. (MIKE) WALSH, *CEO of Houston conglomerate Tenneco, in Fortune in 1992, describing turnarounds he led at Union Pacific Railroad and Tenneco, having been brought in as an outsider CEO in both cases.*

There's no leader of a turnaround who's a beloved leader.... It's impossible to run a leveraged corporation like camp.

> LINDA WACHNER, *CEO of intimate-apparel firm Warnaco, in Fortune in 1993.*

When I became CEO of DLJ, it took a year and a half before I was able to consolidate my authority. It's a wonder the patient didn't die while office politics raged.... [At Equitable] I asked for the total support of the board. Once I got it, I could cut through the red tape, abolish committees, and act decisively.

> RICHARD (DICK) JENRETTE, *who steered securities firm Donaldson Lufkin Jenrette through a recession after becoming CEO in 1973, and later turned around DLJ's parent, U.S. insurer Equitable, quoted in* Fortune *in 1996.*

When you step into a turnaround situation, you can safely assume four things: morale is low, fear is high, the good people are halfway out the door, and the slackers are hiding.

> NINA DISESA, *chairwoman of ad agency McCann-Erickson, in the late 1990s.*

I said: "Tomorrow I will be in my office at four AM and work twenty-four hours if necessary. Come and see me. I don't want to know just what the problems are. I want to know what we're going to do to fix them. And if you're not part of the solution, I will do it myself, but I will take part of your salary."

> DOMENICO DE SOLE, *CEO of Florence-based fashion marketer Gucci Group, in the* New York Times *in 2002, on his first-day instructions to staff at the troubled company, where he led a turnaround in the 1990s.*

The best way to make a silk purse from a sow's ear is to start with a silk sow.

> NORMAN AUGUSTINE, *CEO of U.S. defense contractor Martin Marietta, in 1994, on why many restructurings fail.*

Wealth

Here we are sweetheart: two trucks, five cars, a retinue of servants, a beautiful property, all for one man. Why should there not be storms and uproar from the underdog?

> SIR JOSEPH WESLEY FLAVELLE, *Toronto-based operator of the British Empire's largest pork-packing enterprise in the early 20th century and often scorned by the populist press as a plutocrat, to his wife while preparing for their annual sojourn at a country retreat.*

If you destroy the leisure class, you destroy civilization.

> J. P. MORGAN, *U.S. financier, testifying before a U.S. Senate committee early in the 20th century, cited in John Kenneth Galbraith's,* The Culture of Contentment *(1992). Asked later to identify the leisure class, Morgan told reporters: "All those who can afford to hire a maid."*

Why, just think of it—Mr. Morgan was not even a wealthy man!

> JOHN D. ROCKEFELLER SR., *in 1913, on learning that the recently deceased J. P. Morgan left an estate of just $80 million.*

If a man saves $15 a week and invests in good common stocks...at the end of twenty years, he will have at least $80,000 and...$400 a month. He will be rich. And because income can do that, I am firm in my belief that anyone not only can be rich, but ought to be rich.

> **JOHN T. RASKOB**, *U.S. financier who played a leading role in building General Motors in the early 20th century.*

There's only one way—use this right now.

> **NATHAN ROTHSCHILD**, *investment banker, drawing a pistol from his desk drawer when a wealthy friend asked how he could be sure to retain his fortune until death.*

Gentlemen prefer bonds.

> **ANDREW MELLON**, *Pittsburgh industrialist and U.S. treasury secretary during the Roaring Twenties.*

Behavior that would be branded as bad taste or bad manners or simply bad by us ordinary mortals becomes a charming idiosyncrasy or eccentricity if one is a genius or has $ jillions.

> **MALCOLM S. FORBES**, *U.S. publisher, in* Forbes *magazine in 1968.*

To turn $100 into $110 is work. To turn $100 million into $110 million is inevitable.

> **EDGAR BRONFMAN SR.**, *CEO of liquor giant Seagram, in the 1970s, on the impact of compound interest on his family fortune.*

REALITY CHECK

Money is to the fore now. It is the romance, the poetry of our age.

WILLIAM DEAN HOWELLS, *The Rise of Silas Lapham (1885)*

Having wealth is unjustified, but the Rockefellers justify it by doing good. I had to cut through all this and understand that there is no rational justification for my family having the amount of money that it has, and that the only honest thing to say in defense of it is that we like having the money and the present social system allows us to keep it.

STEVEN ROCKEFELLER, *beneficiary of John D. Rockefeller's Standard Oil wealth, in Peter Collier and David Horowitz's,* The Rockefellers *(1983).*

People look at me differently now. The mailman, the lady at the dry cleaners—they look at me with a price tag. I see it in their eyes. When you have a lot of money, you're looked at as a freak. I'm a financial freak. I was closet rich until this thing was published. Now I'm out of the closet.

LESLIE HERBERT WEXNER, *founder and CEO of U.S. apparel retailer The Limited, in 1983, on being included in the* Forbes *400 list of the wealthiest Americans.*

What William Clay Ford would like to say to all those ambitious Young Turks who dream of making that *Forbes* list is that being rich can screw up their lives.

> **WILLIAM CLAY (BILL) FORD**, *grandson of Henry Ford and future CEO of Ford Motor, in 1988.*

A strong part of me keeps saying, "My God, the money just came to me; maybe it could disappear someday."

> **PETER BRONFMAN**, *minor scion of the Seagram dynasty, whose hired hands turned his modest inheritance into a conglomerate that at its peak in the late 1980s had assets of about $18 billion and employed sixty-four thousand people.*

Average sex is better than being a billionaire.

> **TED TURNER**, *U.S. broadcasting mogul, in* Business Week *in 1997, on the relative value of great wealth.*

If you were a jerk before, you'll be a bigger jerk with a billion dollars.

> **WARREN BUFFETT**, *CEO of Berkshire Hathaway, in* Forbes *in 1997.*

Have you ever been homeless? Have you ever had everything you have in your hands, a carrier bag, and the pockets of your anorak? Well I have.

> **FELIX DENNIS**, *British publisher* (Maxim, Mac User, Personal Computer World), *in 1999, unapologetic about flaunting his wealth. In 2002, Dennis began planting a thirty thousand–acre broad-leaf forest in middle England, which he called the Forest of Dennis.*

Workaholism

If you work twelve hours a day, you finally get to be boss so you can put in sixteen to eighteen hours a day.

> **DONALD KENDALL**, *who became CEO of PepsiCo in 1963 at age forty-two.*

What you do on Saturdays is what puts you ahead of the competition.

> **CURTIS LEROY CARLSON**, *founder of Minneapolis-based conglomerate Carlson Cos., owner of the TGIF (Thank Goodness It's Friday) restaurant chain.*

Most people have an overblown view of how many hours I work.... I'm probably more like seventy average [hours].... You can get weeks where I'll put in over ninety. I mean, I assume you don't count reading business magazines, the [Wall Street] Journal or the Economist.

> **BILL GATES**, *co-founder of Microsoft, cited in Stephen Manes and Paul Andrews's,* Gates: How Microsoft's Mogul Reinvented an Industry—And Made Himself the Richest Man in America *(1993). In his company's early years, Gates's work habits and constant worrying often resulted in insomnia. "He doesn't get enough sleep at night," said one of Gates' colleagues, "and then during the day he could sleep instantly. He'd crawl under a desk. He'd crawl under chairs at the airport and fall asleep. People would lose him."*

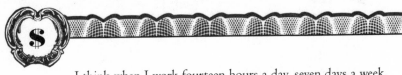

I think when I work fourteen hours a day, seven days a week, I get lucky.

> **ARMAND HAMMER**, *U.S. industrialist and longtime CEO of Occidental Petroleum, in M in 1984.*

The pace of work these days isn't easy to live with, but welcome to the Nineties. Intel didn't create this world; we're just supplying the tools with which we can all work ourselves to death.

> **ANDREW S. GROVE**, *CEO of Intel, the world's leading maker of semiconductors, in the 1990s.*